Academic Vocabulary Practice
Grade 3

Credits

Content Editor: Christine Schwab

Copy Editor: Julie B. Killian

Visit *carsondellosa.com* for correlations to Common Core, state, national, and Canadian provincial standards.

Carson-Dellosa Publishing, LLC
PO Box 35665
Greensboro, NC 27425 USA
carsondellosa.com

IsBN 978-1-4838-1120-8
01-135141151

Table of Contents

Introduction

The Academic Vocabulary Practice Series

Research shows that a firm knowledge of academic vocabulary is one of the strongest indicators of students' success in the content areas. Academic Vocabulary Practice is a series that provides students with the resources they need to build crucial vocabulary skills for success in school. The series promotes and supports literacy in: math, science, technology, language arts, social studies, geography, civics and economics, and art. The reproducible pages are designed to give students extra practice using academic vocabulary. These word lists focus on subject-specific words that often challenge students because they may rarely encounter these words in everyday use.

The books align with the Common Core State Standards by offering systematic practice and usage of many of the academic and domain-specific words and phrases. Teaching vocabulary to meet the Common Core State Standards is an essential component of any standards-based curriculum.

Reproducible Pages in This Book

This book presents 200+ subject-specific words that are organized by content area. Ample opportunity is given to help students learn and connect with the vocabulary in a variety of ways.

- The *Vocabulary Four Square* on page 4 is an essential organizer that helps students learn new words by stating word meanings in their own words, drawing pictures to represent the words, engaging with peers in word discussions, and creating context for words.

- The *Explore a Word* activities let students focus on one word at a time to create associations.

- The *Compare Words* activities show students how two related words are alike and different in meaning.

- The *Make Connections* pages help students understand the relationships between words that are commonly presented together.

- The *Play with Words* activities provide review in a more playful but effective learning format.

Special Features

The *Game Ideas and Suggestions* section includes ideas for using the flash cards (offered online) and game templates for small group or whole group activities. The *Student Dictionary* pages are organized by content area and support the activity pages in each section.

Online Support

To further enhance student learning, the 200+ vocabulary words are available in flash card format online at *activities.carsondellosa.com*. These will provide opportunities for additional practice and other peer activities.

Vocabulary Four Square

Use the Vocabulary Four Square to practice new words in this book.

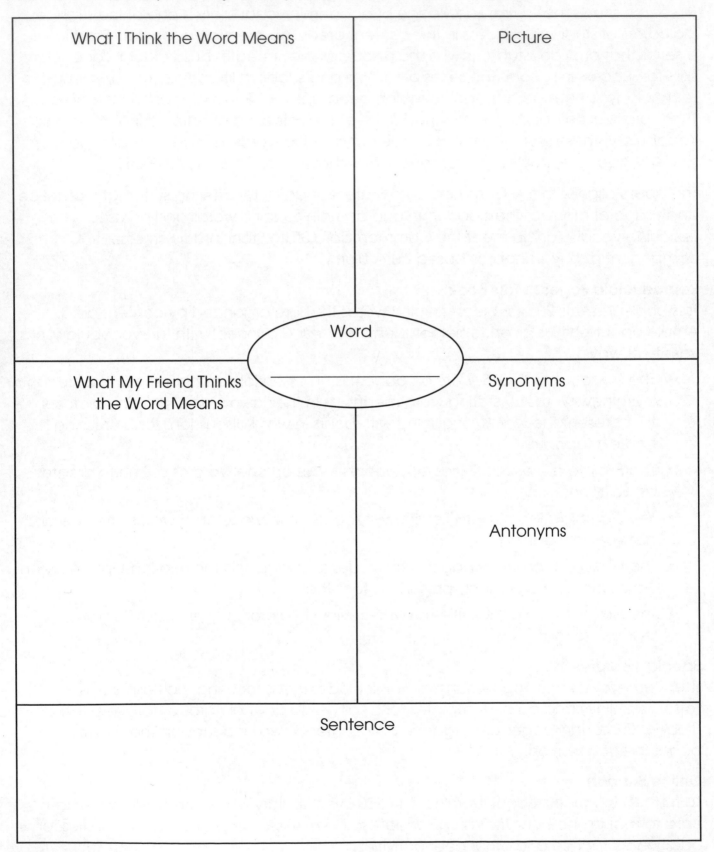

What I Think the Word Means

Picture

Word
_____

What My Friend Thinks
the Word Means

Synonyms

Antonyms

Sentence

 Academic Vocabulary Practice • Grade 3 • CD-104808

Important Math
Words You Need to Know

Use this list to keep track of how well you know the new words.

0 = Don't Know   1 = Know Somewhat   2 = Know Well

___ algorithm

___ angle

___ area

___ bar graph

___ capacity

___ common noun

___ decimal point

___ denominator

___ diagonal

___ digit

___ dividend

___ division

___ divisor

___ equilateral triangle

___ equivalent

___ estimate

___ factor

___ fraction

___ hexagon

___ line segment

___ measurement

___ multiple

___ multiplication

___ numerator

___ octagon

___ parallel

___ pentagon

___ perimeter

___ perpendicular

___ pictograph

___ polygon

___ product

___ quotient

___ rectangle

___ remainder

___ right triangle

___ tally chart

___ volume

Explore a Word

Read the paragraph. Think about the meaning of the **bold** word.

An **algorithm** is a step-by-step way to solve a problem. An algorithm works every time. A simple algorithm for adding three-digit numbers is shown here:

	134
	+227
1. Add 100s	300
2. Add 10s	50
3. Add 1s	+11
4. Add partial sums	361

1. What do you think the word means? Write your idea.

   algorithm: _____

   _____

2. Write a sentence with the word **algorithm**. Show what it means.

   _____

   _____

3. Check the meaning of **algorithm** in the Student Dictionary.

4. If your sentence in step 2 matches the meaning, put a ✓ after it. If your sentence does not match the meaning, write a better sentence.

   _____

   _____

5. Write an **algorithm** for the problem and solve it.

	324
	+165

Compare Words

Look at the picture and read the caption. Think about the meaning of each **bold** word. Then, check the Student Dictionary.

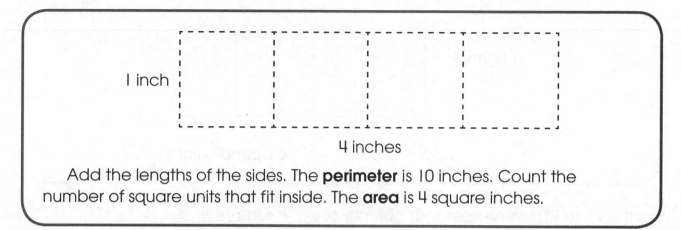

I inch

4 inches

Add the lengths of the sides. The **perimeter** is 10 inches. Count the number of square units that fit inside. The **area** is 4 square inches.

Write the words *perimeter* and *area* where they fit in each sentence. Then, draw a picture with labels to show the measurements that are described.

1. We rode our bikes 4 miles on a path around the _____ of the park. The _____ of the park is 1 square mile.

2. One side of a square rug is 3 feet long. The _____ of the rug is 12 feet. The _____ of the rug Is 9 square feet.

3. The _____ of the sheet of paper is 15 square inches. The _____ of the paper is 16 inches.

Compare Words

Look at the picture and read the labels. Think about the meaning of each **bold** word. Then, check the Student Dictionary.

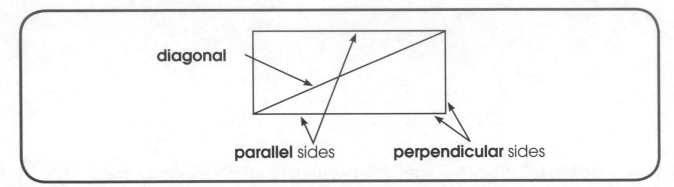

Circle the word in parentheses that completes each sentence.

1. A floor and a roof are (diagonal/parallel) to each other.

2. A floor and a wall are (diagonal/perpendicular) to each other.

3. Connect opposite corners with a (diagonal/parallel) line.

4. (Diagonal/Parallel) lines are slanted.

5. A square has sides that are (diagonal/perpendicular).

6. A square has two equal sets of (parallel/perpendicular) sides.

7. Two (diagonal/perpendicular) sides of the roof meet at the top.

Look around. What perpendicular things do you see? Do you see diagonals or parallels? Write an example of each.

8. perpendicular:_____

9. diagonal:_____

10. parallel: _____

Academic Vocabulary Practice • Grade 3 • CD-104808

Compare Words

Read the paragraph. Think about the meaning of each **bold** term. Then, check the Student Dictionary.

> A **bar graph** uses bars of different heights to show information. A **pictograph** uses symbols or pictures to show information. A **tally chart** uses tally marks to keep count.

Gather information from at least five classmates to fill in the charts.

1. Bar Graph: Our Favorite Sports

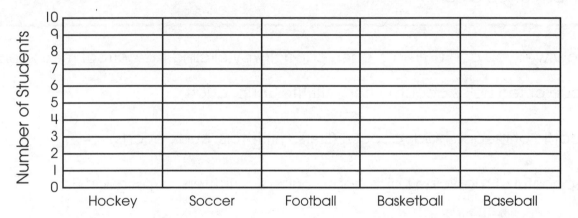

2. Pictograph: Our Favorite Flavors

Ice Cream Flavors	Number of Students
strawberry	
chocolate	
vanilla	
wild cherry	

3. Tally Chart: Our Favorite Colors

Color	Tally	Number of Students

Make Connections

Read the paragraph. Think about the meaning of each **bold** word. Then, check the Student Dictionary.

> **Capacity** is the **volume** of materials a container can hold in liquid units. This kind of **measurement** can be **estimated** once you know more about liquid amounts.
>
> large soft drink bottle = 1 liter (L)
>
> 20 drops of water = 1 milliliter (mL)
> cup of coffee = 1 cup
> box of ice cream = 1 quart

Show how well you can estimate each capacity by circling the correct measurement.

1. A cup of tea holds about 1 (liter, milliliter, cup, quart).

2. A bottle of bleach holds about 4 (liters, milliliters, cups, quarts).

3. A spoonful of medicine holds about 2 (liters, milliliters, cups, quarts).

4. A can of paint holds about 4 (liters, milliliters, cups, quarts).

5. A punch bowl holds 3 (liters, milliliters, cups, quarts).

6. A goldfish bowl holds about 2 (liters, milliliters, cups, quarts) of water.

7. A bottle of glue holds about half a (liter, milliliter, cup, quart).

8. A small pan of hot water holds 3 or 4 (liters, milliliters, cups, quarts).

9. An aquarium fish tank holds about 900 (liters, milliliters, cups, quarts) of water.

10. Some salt shakers hold 50 (liters, milliliters, cups, quarts) of salt.

Make Connections

Read the example and the sentence. Think about the meaning of each **bold** term. Then, check the Student Dictionary.

> $132.24
>
> The **digit** 2 stands for two dollars before the **decimal point**. To the right of the decimal point, the digit 2 stands for twenty cents.

Follow each instruction.

1. Write the digits 3, 5, and 7 in order. Circle the digit that is in the tens place.

   _____

2. Use numbers to write the amount ten dollars and fifty-two cents. Circle the decimal point.

   _____

3. Write a number in which the digit 6 stands for six tenths.

   _____

4. Do amounts become greater to the left of a decimal point, or do they become less? Explain your answer with an example.

   _____

 **Look It Up!**

The word *digit* has more than one meaning. Use a classroom dictionary to find the meaning that fits with each picture. Complete the sentences.

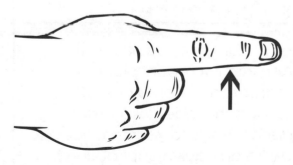

1. A digit is a _____.

2. A digit is a _____.

Make Connections

Read the sentence. Think about the meaning of each **bold** word. Then, check the Student Dictionary.

> In the **fraction** $\frac{3}{4}$, the **numerator** is 3, and the **denominator** is 4. **Equivalent** fractions have the same value even if they look different.

Underline the correct ending to each sentence.

1. The numerator is the number
   A. above the line in a fraction.
   B. below the line in a fraction.

2. The denominator tells how rnany
   A. equal parts are in the whole.
   B. numerators are in the whole.

3. Equivalent fractions are
   A. equal to each other.
   B. small fractions.

4. A numerator shows how many
   A. parts of the whole are counted.
   B. equal parts are in the whole.

5. The denominator is 2 in
   A. the fraction $\frac{3}{4}$.

   B. the fraction $\frac{1}{2}$.

 Challenge!

Draw a picture of a cracker that is broken into two equal pieces. Write a fraction to name one of the pieces. Add the labels *numerator* and *denominator* to your fraction. Then, write an equivalent fraction that describes one of the cracker pieces.

Academic Vocabulary Practice • Grade 3 • CD-104808

Make Connections

Look at the pictures and read the captions. Think about the meaning of each **bold** term. Then, check the Student Dictionary.

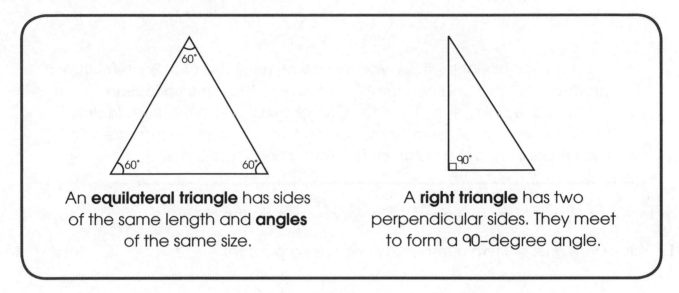

An **equilateral triangle** has sides of the same length and **angles** of the same size.

A **right triangle** has two perpendicular sides. They meet to form a 90-degree angle.

Circle the picture that answers each question.

1. Which picture shows a right triangle?

    A. 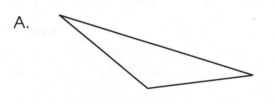   B.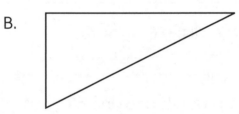

2. Which picture shows an angle?

    A. 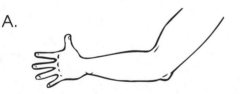   B.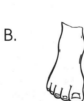

3. Which picture shows an equilateral triangle.

    A.    B.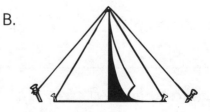

Make Connections

Read the paragraph. Think about the meaning of each **bold** word. Then, check the Student Dictionary.

> 5, 10, 15, 20, 25
>
> When you count by fives, you are saying **multiples** of 5. Each multiple is a **product** of 5 and another number. When you learn **multiplication** facts, you are learning lists of multiples. Multiples are different from **factors**. Multiples are what you get after multiplying two numbers. Factors are what you can multiply to get a number. Two factors of 10 are 2 and 5.

Circle *Yes* or *No* for each question. Write your reason on the line.

1. When you multiply two numbers, do you get a product?   Yes   No

   _____

2. Is multiplication like subtraction?   Yes   No

   _____

3. Is 12 a multiple of 2?   Yes   No

   _____

4. Is 12 a product of 6 and 6?   Yes   No

   _____

5. Is 3 a factor of 12?   Yes   No

   _____

6. Is a multiple of a number less than that number?   Yes   No

   _____

Follow the directions.

7. List ten multiples of 6.

   _____

8. List twelve factors of 60.

   _____

Make Connections

Read the example and the paragraph. Think about the meaning of each **bold** word. Then, check the Student Dictionary

$$\frac{4\ r2}{3\overline{)14}}$$

In this **division** problem, the amount you want to divide, or 14, is called the **dividend**. The amount of parts you want to divide it by, or 3, is called the **divisor**. The answer is called the **quotient**, or 4, with a **remainder** of 2.

Follow each instruction.

1. Circle all of the examples that show division.

    $15 \div 3$ $15 + 15$ $7 \div 4$ $4\overline{)20}$

2. Three friends want to share 7 grapes. Write a division problem to show the number of grapes each friend will get. Label each part of the division problem with a vocabulary word.

3. Look at the example at the top of this page. Use words and numbers to explain why the quotient is 4 r2.

    _____

    _____

 **Challenge!**

Read the sentence. Write or draw to show what it means.

The quotient in a division problem shows the number of equal parts.

Make Connections

Read the paragraph. Think about the meaning of each **bold** word. Then, check the Student Dictionary.

> Three or more **line segments** connect to form a shape called a **polygon**. One kind of polygon is a **rectangle**. A rectangle has 4 sides and 4 right angles. A **pentagon** is another kind of polygon. It has 5 sides. A **hexagon** has 6 sides. An **octagon** has 8 sides.

Label each polygon.

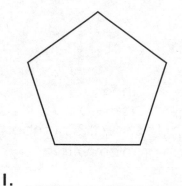

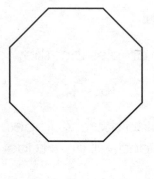

1. _____

2. _____

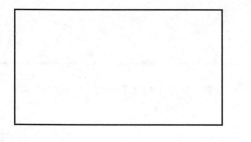

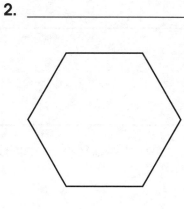

3. _____

4. _____

★ Challenge!

Look at the shape. Is it a polygon? Write *Yes* or *No*. Then, write your reason.

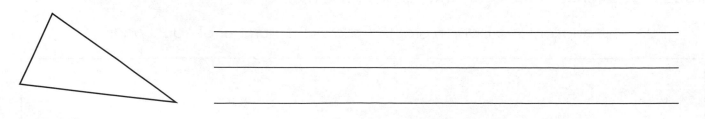

Play with Words

Letter by Letter

Choose the word that fits with each clue. Write it letter by letter. Some letters will be inside circles.

fraction	hexagon	multiples
polygons	product	quotient

1. $15 \div 3 = ?$ __ __ __ __ __ Ⓞ __ __

2. [hexagon shape]   __ __ Ⓞ __ __ __ __

3. A triangle and a rectangle   Ⓞ __ __ __ __ __ __ __

4. 3, 6, 9, 12, 15   __ __ __ __ __ __ Ⓞ __

5. $10 \times 5 = ?$ __ Ⓞ __ __ __ __ __

6. $\frac{12}{13}$ __ __ __ __ Ⓞ __ __ __

Write the circled letters in order. You will find a word that completes the message.

You must be an __ __ __ __ __ __!

Play with Words

Code Words

Choose the word or words that fits in each sentence. Circle the letter.

1. The number 4 is a ___.
    f digit
    g fraction
    h decimal point

2. A polygon with five sides is a ___.
    h right triangle
    i pentagon
    j octagon

3. The letter **L** has ___ line segments.
    e diagonal
    f octagon
    g perpendicular

4. The fraction $\frac{2}{3}$ has the ___ 2.
    s denominator
    t quotient
    u numerator

5. A ___ cuts a rectangle into two right triangles.
    r diagonal
    s measurement
    t perimeter

6. ___ is measured in square units.
    c Perimeter
    d Angle
    e Area

Write the circled letters in order. You will find a word for a number or a shape. The word also tells what math students do.

_____

Academic Vocabulary Practice • Grade 3 • CD-104808

Important Science Words You Need to Know

Use this list to keep track of how well you know the new words.

0 = Don't Know   1 = Know Somewhat   2 = Know Well

___ adaptations

___ asteroid

___ astronomer

___ axis

___ carnivore

___ comet

___ condense

___ decomposer

___ ecosystem

___ evaporate

___ food web

___ gas

___ habitat

___ herbivore

___ humidity

___ liquid

___ matter

___ nutrient

___ orbit

___ omnivore

___ overheated

___ perspire

___ plasma

___ precipitation

___ predator

___ prey

___ producer

___ reproduce

___ revolve

___ rotate

___ solar system

___ solid

___ species

___ tilt

___ water cycle

___ water vapor

Explore a Word

Read the paragraph. Think about the meaning of the **bold** word. Then, check the Student Dictionary.

> Plants and animals have many adaptations to help them stay alive. For example, a cactus has roots that spread out to collect water in the ground. Its roots are an **adaptation** that allows the cactus to live in dry areas. Another example of an adaptation is an eagle's sharp eyesight. This adaptation helps the bird hunt small animals when it flies high above the ground.

Fill in the web to show your ideas about adaptations.

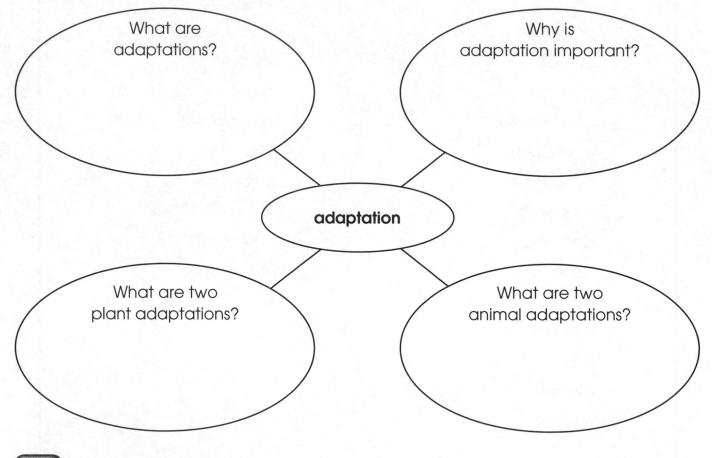

Word Alert!

A suffix is a word part added to the end of a word. The suffix *-ation* is added to the base word *adapt*. Complete the sentence with *adapt* and *adaptation*.

Thick fur is one (1.) _____ that helps mammals

(2.) _____ to cold weather.

Compare Words

Read the paragraph. Think about the meaning of each **bold** word. Then, check the Student Dictionary.

> Some animals are **herbivores**. They eat fruits, seeds, grasses, and plants. These animals are eaten by **carnivores**.

Circle the word in parentheses that completes each sentence.

1. Lions and tigers are (herbivores/carnivores).

2. Cows and sheep are (herbivores/carnivores).

3. Owls are (herbivores/carnivores) that catch and eat mice.

4. Some kinds of (herbivores/carnivores) live in herds that roam over grasslands to graze.

5. Wolves are (herbivores/carnivores) that hunt in groups called packs.

 **Challenge!**

The word part -*vore* is in *herbivore* and *carnivore*. What do you think this word part means? What do you think an **omnivore** is? Check your ideas in a classroom dictionary. Then, draw pictures to show what you have learned about the words *herbivore*, *carnivore*, and *omnivore*.

Compare Words

Read the paragraph. Think about the meaning of each **bold** word. Then, check the Student Dictionary.

> Have you ever seen a pet cat crouch and move slowly before pouncing on a toy? In the wild, a cat is a **predator** that hides and moves slowly to sneak up on its **prey**.

Read each sentence. Copy each underlined word and label it *predator* or *prey*.

1. A <u>spider</u> spins a web to trap <u>insects</u>.

    _____

2. <u>Deer</u> are fast enough to outrun <u>wolves</u>.

    _____

3. Watch a <u>robin</u> pull an <u>earthworm</u> out of the ground.

    _____

4. A <u>polar bear</u> hunts for <u>seals</u> under the ice.

    _____

5. <u>Sharks</u> are food for some kinds of <u>seals</u>.

    _____

Make Connections

Read the paragraphs. Think about the meaning of each **bold** word. Then, check the Student Dictionary.

> Living things and nonliving things are connected in every **ecosystem**. For example, sunlight, soil, water, and air are nonliving things. They are used by plants to produce food. Plants are **producers**. Herbivores eat plants, and then carnivores eat herbivores.
>
> When plants and animals die, their remains are broken down into **nutrients** that return to the soil. The living things that break down the material are called **decomposers**. Most decomposers are too tiny to see.

Underline the correct ending to each sentence.

1. An example of an ecosystem is
   A. a pond.
   B. a swimming pool.

2. An example of a producer is
   A. soil.
   B. a tree.

3. Producers use sunlight to
   A. make water warm.
   B. make food.

4. We can see the work of decomposers in
   A. rotting fruit.
   B. a plant bud.

5. Decomposers are needed to
   A. enrich the soil for producers.
   B. provide a source of food for carnivores.

6. Nutrients are added to soil when ___.
   A. it is soaked with water.
   B. animals decompose and plants die.

Make Connections

Read the paragraph. Think about the meaning of each **bold** word. Then, check the Student Dictionary.

> The living things in a **habitat** must find food, stay safe, and **reproduce**. The **species** that share a habitat form **food webs**. Plants are the start of every food chain. They produce food for all kinds of animals. Plant-eating animals, in turn, are eaten by other animals. Every habitat has food webs that show connections among the species.

Complete each sentence with a vocabulary word.

1. An oak tree produces acorns so that the tree will _____.

2. Fish in the deep ocean live in a dark, cold _____.

3. A caterpillar eats a leaf. A bird eats the caterpillar. The leaf, the caterpillar, and the bird form a chain that is part of a bigger _____.

4. The northern flying squirrel and the southern flying squirrel look alike. But, they are two different _____.

5. A male and a female insect must be of the same species to _____.

6. In the habitat of a freshwater lake, green plants, insects, fish, birds, reptiles, and mammals are all linked in a _____.

 **Challenge!**

Choose a habitat. On another sheet of paper, draw a food chain from that habitat.

Make Connections

Read the paragraph. Think about the meaning of each **bold** word. Then, check the Student Dictionary.

> Air is **matter**. Water is matter. The sun is matter. You and everything around you are made of matter. Matter is anything that takes up space and has weight. It can be in the form of a **solid**, a **liquid**, a **gas**, or **plasma**.

Read each question. Circle the answer.

1. What form of matter is inside a balloon?   solid   liquid   gas   plasma

2. What form of matter is orange juice?   solid   liquid   gas   plasma

3. What form of matter is rain?   solid   liquid   gas   plasma

4. What form of matter is the sun?   solid   liquid   gas   plasma

5. What form of matter is an ice cube?   solid   liquid   gas   plasma

6. What form of matter spreads out to fill a room?   solid   liquid   gas   plasma

7. What form of matter keeps its shape?   solid   liquid   gas   plasma

8. What form of matter is a gas that has been energized?   solid   liquid   gas   plasma

 # Look It Up!

We use one meaning of *matter* to talk about science. We use another meaning of *matter* in everyday language. Look up *matter* in a classroom dictionary. Write the meaning that fits with each phrase below. Use your own words to tell what the phrase means.

1. a matter to discuss: _____

   _____

2. a state of matter: _____

   _____

Make Connections

Read the paragraphs. Think about the meaning of each **bold** term. Then, check the Student Dictionary.

> Did you drink some water today? The water you drank was extremely old—as old as Earth itself! Water moves from one place to another through a process called the **water cycle**.
>
> Water is a liquid in oceans, rivers, and other bodies of water. The sun's heat causes water to **evaporate** and change into a gas. The gas rises. As it cools, the gas **condenses** back into a liquid. It falls as rain or another form of **precipitation**.

Add labels to explain what is shown in this diagram. Use all of the vocabulary words.

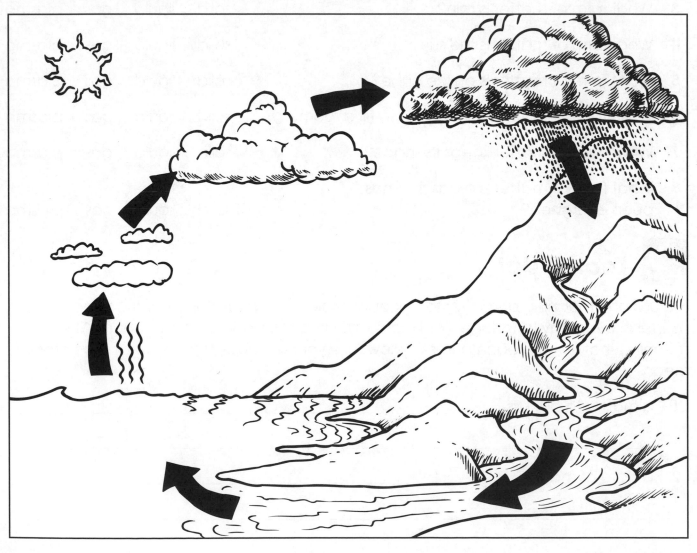

     Academic Vocabulary Practice • Grade 3 • CD-104808

Make Connections

Read the paragraphs. Think about the meaning of each **bold** term. Then, check the Student Dictionary.

> On a hot day, your body **perspires** through tiny holes in your skin. The liquid water on your skin changes into a gas called **water vapor**. The water vapor pulls heat away from your body and into the air. This is the body's way of cooling itself so that it does not become **overheated**. But, the liquid water does not evaporate if the air holds a lot of **humidity**. Then, your skin stays hot and sticky.
>
> Remember that when you perspire, you are losing water that your body needs. So, be sure to drink plenty of water on hot days!

Use your ideas to complete each sentence with one or more words that make sense.

1. Water vapor is _____ in the form of a gas.

2. A body that cannot _____ could become overheated.

3. I can tell that I am perspiring when _____ on my skin.

4. On a day with high humidity, the air _____ water vapor.

5. To avoid overheating, a person should _____ and find shade.

Make Connections

Look at the diagram and read the caption. Think about the meaning of each **bold** word. Then, check the Student Dictionary.

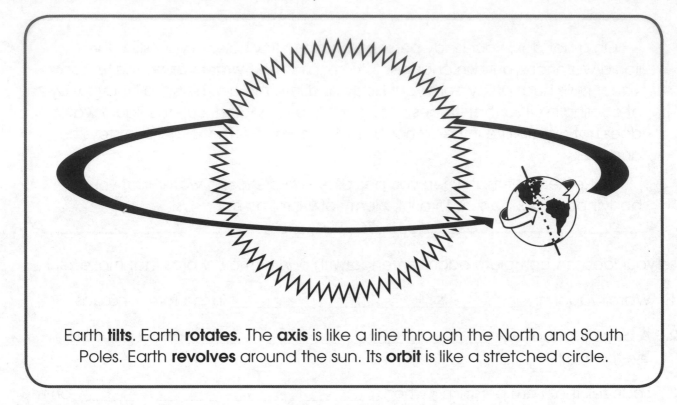

Earth **tilts**. Earth **rotates**. The **axis** is like a line through the North and South Poles. Earth **revolves** around the sun. Its **orbit** is like a stretched circle.

Use the vocabulary words to complete the paragraph.

It takes a year for Earth to complete its (1.) _____ around the

sun. The planet is not straight, but (2.) _____ instead. This means that

Earth's northern half and southern half get different amounts of sunlight during the year.

As a result, Earth has seasons. Earth (3.) _____ around an imaginary

line called the (4.) _____. Earth completes a spin every 24 hours, or a

night and a day.

Make Connections

Read the paragraph. Think about the meaning of each **bold** word. Then, check the Student Dictionary.

> Our **solar system** has the sun at its center. The solar system also has planets and their moons. **Astronomers** study other bodies in the solar system too. **Asteroids** are much smaller than planets. They are made of rock or metals. Most asteroids orbit the sun between Mars and Jupiter. Icy **comets** make long, oval orbits from the far edges of the solar system.

Circle *Yes* or *No* for each question. Write your reason on the line.

1. Is a comet like a planet?   Yes   No

    _____

2. Is the solar system part of Earth?   Yes   No

    _____

3. Do all bodies in the solar system orbit the sun?   Yes   No

    _____

4. Are astronomers astronauts?   Yes   No

    _____

5. Is an asteroid a moon?   Yes   No

    _____

🔍 Look It Up!

The vocabulary words *asteroid* and *astronomer* begin with the same letters. They come from Greek words that have to do with stars. Look up the words in a classroom dictionary. Circle the words that have to do with stars or space.

> asterisk   asthma   astound   astronaut   astronomy

Play with Words

Code Words

Choose the word or words that complete each sentence. Circle the letter.

1. A plant eater is a ___.
   d carnivore
   e herbivore
   f predator

2. Earth ___ around the sun.
   n revolves
   o tilts
   p axis

3. Seashores and forests are ___.
   c species
   d nutrients
   e ecosystems

4. Small mammals are often ___.
   r prey
   s producers
   t extinct

5. Water vapor forms when liquid water ___.
   e humidity
   f condenses
   g evaporates

6. ___ orbit the sun.
   x Astronomers
   y Comets
   z Solar systems

Write the circled letters in order. You will find a word that completes the sentence.

Scientists study matter and _____.

Play with Words

Vocabulary Crossword Puzzle

Use the clues to solve the crossword puzzle.

ACROSS
5   Imaginary line through a planet
6   All plants
7   Snow, rain, hail
8   Eaters and the eaten (two words)

DOWN
1   Hawks, lions, sharks
2   A space scientist
3   Groups of living things
4   A community of living things

Important Technology
Words You Need to Know

Use this list to keep track of how well you know the new words.

0 = Don't Know   1 = Know Somewhat   2 = Know Well

___ brainstorm

___ browser

___ engineer

___ gear

___ home page

___ Internet

___ inventor

___ pulley

___ ramp

___ recycle

___ reduce

___ reuse

___ simple machine

___ surf

___ technology

___ website

___ wheel and axle

Explore a Word

Read the paragraphs. Think about the meaning of each **bold** word. Then, check the Student Dictionary.

> Where can you find **technology**? Just look around you. Technology is anything that people have made to solve a problem. A pencil, an eraser, a carpet, and a computer are all technologies.
>
> How do people come up with technologies? First, they ask, "Can we make something to solve this problem?" Next, they **brainstorm** with others to come up with ideas for solving the problem.

Fill in the chart to show your understanding of the word *brainstorm*.

1. What is brainstorming?	2. Why is *brainstorm* a good name?
3. How is brainstorming different from thinking?	**4.** What do people do after they brainstorm?
5. Name as many forms of technology as you can, that you see in your classroom or home.	

Compare Words

Read the paragraph. Think about the meaning of each **bold** word. Then, check the Student Dictionary.

> **Inventors** use their knowledge of science to think of ideas for new products. **Engineers** use science to figure out how to make new products.

Circle the word in parentheses that completes each sentence.

1. A government grants a patent to any (inventor/engineer) of a new product. A patent is the sole right to make or sell a product.

2. Thomas Edison had more than 1,000 patents for products. He was the most famous (inventor/engineer) of his time.

3. Some (inventors/engineers) design bridges and tunnels.

4. The people who design video games are called software (inventors/engineers).

5. The Wright brothers were the (inventors/engineers) of the first motor-powered airplane. Before their first successful flight, they had been (inventors/engineers) who always worked with machines.

 **Challenge!**

You can see the base word *engine* in *engineer*. What does an engine have to do with the field of engineering? Use a classroom dictionary to find the answer. Write it below.

_____

_____

Make Connections

Read the paragraph. Think about the meaning of each **bold** word. Then, check the Student Dictionary.

> Use a **browser** to reach a **website** on the **Internet**. When kids **surf** the Internet, they should only stay on trusted websites. You can usually tell from the **home page** what a website is about. If the home page does not look safe or appropriate, go to another website, tell an adult, or leave the Internet.

Complete each sentence with your own ideas.

1. My computer is connected to the Internet. That means I can _____

    _____ .

2. I type an address in the field displayed by the browser. The browser quickly _____

    _____ .

3. When I surf the Internet, I like to look for websites about _____ .

4. The browser takes charge of all links on a web page. If I click on _____

    _____ .

5. The Internet covers the world. That means that I might _____

    _____ .

6. The browser on our school computers is called _____

    _____ .

Word Alert!

The prefix *inter-* means "between." Underline each word with *inter-* in the sentence below. Use your own words to tell what the sentence means. Do not use any of the underlined words in your sentence.

The Internet has many interactive games for interconnected users.

_____

_____

Make Connections

Read the paragraph. Think about the meaning of each **bold** term. Then, check the Student Dictionary.

> Movers use a **ramp** to load heavy furniture into a truck. Like other **simple machines**, a ramp makes work easier.

Circle *Yes* or *No* for each question. Write your reason on the line.

1. Do all simple machines have moving parts?   Yes   No

   _____

2. Is a car an example of a simple machine?   Yes   No

   _____

3. Does an object on a ramp move a shorter distance
   than an object that is lifted straight up?   Yes   No

   _____

4. Is a ladder an example of a ramp?   Yes   No

   _____

5. Must you use force to move an object up a ramp?   Yes   No

   _____

Draw a picture of a ramp. Write a caption to tell how it is used.

Make Connections

Look at the pictures and read the captions. Think about the meaning of each **bold** term. Then, check the Student Dictionary.

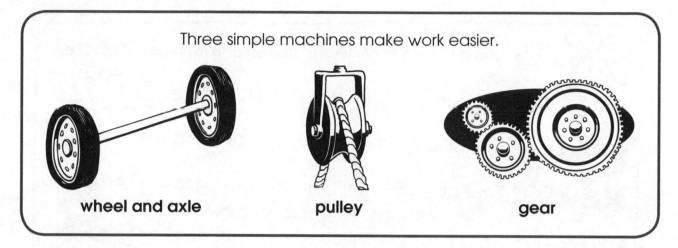

Three simple machines make work easier.

wheel and axle   **pulley**   **gear**

Use the vocabulary words to complete the paragraph.

Some kinds of simple machines are made with wheels. A rod is inserted into the center of a wheel in a (1.) _____. One turn of the axle causes the wheel to move a greater distance than the axle moves. Pulling down on the rope of a (2.) _____ lifts a weight on the other end. Turning one wheel of a (3.) _____ causes the other wheel to turn.

Each item below works because of a simple machine. Write the vocabulary word that names the simple machine.

4. window blinds: _____

5. bicycle chain: _____

6. roller skate: _____

Make Connections

Read the poster. Think about the meaning of each **bold** word. Then, check the Student Dictionary.

> We need a healthy environment. We need to manage our waste. We all can help if we practice the 3 R's!
>
> **Reduce.** Avoid wasteful packaging. Buy and use less stuff.
>
> **Reuse.** Find new uses for things. Buy used items. They can be as good as new ones.
>
> **Recycle.** Don't throw away anything that can be made into something new.

Answer each question.

1. What are three things you try to recycle?

   _____

2. How can you reduce your use of paper and plastic cups?

   _____

3. What are two ways that clothing you have outgrown can be reused?

   _____

   _____

! Word Alert!

The prefix *re-* means "again" in each word below. Use the word *again* as you write a meaning for each word.

4. reuse: _____

5. renew: _____

6. refill: _____

Play with Words

Code Words

Choose the word or words that complete each sentence. Circle the letter.

1. Computers connected worldwide form the ___.
   - c inventor
   - d Internet
   - e browser

2. A ___ raises a flag on a flagpole.
   - d ramp
   - e pulley
   - f gear

3. A tug on a rope is ___.
   - s a force
   - t a pulley
   - u simple machine

4. A wheelchair ramp is a ___.
   - i simple machine
   - j gear
   - k recycle

5. ___ build models to test.
   - e Browsers
   - f Forces
   - g Engineers

6. Can you ___ your use of paper?
   - l reuse
   - m brainstorm
   - n reduce

Write the circled letters in order. You will find a word that answers this question: *What do you call a plan for a new technology?*

a _____

Play with Words

Letter by Letter

Choose the word that fits with each clue. Write it letter by letter. Some letters will be inside circles.

engineer	force	inventor
pulley	recycle	wheel

1. Do this with glass and plastic. ___ ___ ___ Ⓞ ___ ___ ___

2. This is a push or a pull. ___ Ⓞ ___ ___ ___

3. This helps you lift something. ___ Ⓞ ___ ___ ___ ___

4. This is attached to an axle. ___ Ⓞ ___ ___ ___

5. This worker designs software. ___ ___ ___ Ⓞ ___ ___ ___

6. This worker has a new idea. ___ Ⓞ ___ ___ ___ ___ ___ ___

Write the circled letters in order. You will find a message.

___ ___ ___   ___ ___ ___ !

Important Language Arts Words You Need to Know

Use this list to keep track of how well you know the new words.

0 = Don't Know   1 = Know Somewhat   2 = Know Well

___ adjective

___ adverb

___ antonym

___ appendix

___ audience

___ biography

___ character

___ common noun

___ context clue

___ definition

___ dialogue

___ draft

___ edit

___ fact

___ fantasy

___ fiction

___ glossary

___ haiku

___ homophone

___ index

___ journal

___ nonfiction

___ noun

___ opinion

___ plural

___ pourquoi tale

___ prefix

___ proofread

___ proper noun

___ publish

___ quotation marks

___ revise

___ sequence

___ singular

___ suffix

___ synonym

___ verb

Explore a Word

Read the poem and the caption. Think about the meaning of the **bold** word. Then, check the Student Dictionary.

> Listen to the brook
> as it whispers and giggles,
> sharing its secrets.
>
> A **haiku** is a three-line poem. Often, it describes a simple scene in nature. Each line in the poem has a certain number of syllables. There are five syllables in the first line, seven syllables in the second line, and five syllables in the third line.

Follow each instruction.

1. Use your own words to tell what the haiku above is about.

   _____

2. Read the lines below. Underline the one that could be in a haiku.

   A. on a snow-covered tree branch
   B. dogs barking, yipping, leaping, and spinning

3. Write the first line of a haiku about rain.

   _____

4. List three topics you might write about in a haiku.

   _____

5. Draw a picture of something to describe in a haiku. Then, write the haiku.

   [ ]

Compare Words

Read the chart. Think about the meaning of each **bold** word. Then, check the Student Dictionary.

Prefix	Meaning	Examples	**Suffix**	Meaning	Examples
re-	"again"	redo, replay, refill	-er	"someone who does something"	worker, dancer, writer
un-	"not," "the opposite of"	undo, unfair, unbutton	-ly	"in a way that is"	slowly, softly, happily

Follow each instruction.

1. Add the prefix *un-* to the base word *wise*. Write the word and its meaning.

   _____

2. Add the suffix *-er* to the base word *teach*. Write the word and its meaning.

   _____

3. Write the meaning of *reuse*. Write the prefix and the base word in *reuse*.

   _____

4. Write the meaning of *quietly*. Write the base word and the suffix in *quietly*.

   _____

5. Write the three parts in *unfairly*. Label the prefix and the suffix.

   _____

6. Explain the difference between a prefix and a suffix.

   _____

Compare Words

Read the sentences. Think about the meaning of each **bold** word. Then, check the Student Dictionary.

> *Easy* and *simple* are **synonyms**. *Easy* and *hard* are **antonyms**.

Read each sentence. Are the underlined words synonyms or antonyms? Circle the answer.

1. I like <u>hot</u> food, but this rice is too <u>spicy</u>!   synonyms   antonyms

2. The <u>cool</u> air is turning <u>warm</u>.   synonyms   antonyms

3. Should we talk <u>loudly</u> or <u>softly</u>?   synonyms   antonyms

4. Carla <u>smiled</u>, and her friends <u>grinned</u>.   synonyms   antonyms

5. That <u>big</u> house has <u>large</u> windows.   synonyms   antonyms

6. Is the dog's fur <u>short</u> or <u>long</u>?   synonyms   antonyms

7. Turn <u>left</u> first and then <u>right</u>.   synonyms   antonyms

8. The <u>clever</u> fox has a <u>smart</u> plan.   synonyms   antonyms

Q Look It Up!

Prefixes and suffixes are listed in a dictionary. Look up the prefix *anti-* (or *ant-*) in a classroom dictionary. How does its meaning help you remember the meaning of *antonym*?

_____

_____

Compare Words

Read the chart. Think about the meaning of each **bold** word. Then, check the Student Dictionary.

A **noun** is a naming word. It names a person, a place, or a thing.	A **verb** is an action word. It shows what someone or something does or is.
Examples: person, boy, girl, child, doctor, place, city, street, mountain, thing, toy, book, fingernail, shoe	Examples: runs, sits, dances, jumps, talks, helps, asks, reads, wiggles, spins, plays, writes, be, is

Read each sentence. Copy each underlined word and label it *noun* or *verb*.

1. We <u>watched</u> the exciting <u>game</u>.

   _____

2. Six <u>dancers</u> <u>twirled</u> fast!

   _____

3. <u>Cats</u> <u>stretch</u> and <u>yawn</u>.

   _____

4. My <u>mother</u> <u>is</u> a <u>teacher</u>.

   _____

5. The big yellow <u>house</u> <u>sits</u> on a <u>hill</u>.

   _____

 **Challenge!**

Write the meaning of the sentence. Then, explain it to a partner.

The word *verb* is a noun.

_____

_____

Compare Words

Read the chart. Think about the meaning of each **bold** word. Then, check the Student Dictionary.

A **singular** noun names one person, place, or thing.	A **plural** noun names more than one person, place, or thing.
Examples: person, child, girl, boy, place, city, beach, library, thing, toy, daisy, foot, mouse	Examples: people, children, girls, boys, places, cities, beaches, libraries, things, toys, daisies, feet, mice

Read each noun. Write *S* if it is singular. Write *P* if it is plural.

1. women ___

2. house ___

3. dogs ___

4. rabbit ___

5. pennies ___

6. bushes ___

7. glass ___

8. dresses ___

9. chair ___

10. wolves ___

★ Challenge!

Look at each of the numbered nouns above. If the noun is singular, write the plural form. If it is plural, write the singular form.

_____

_____

_____

_____

Compare Words

Read the chart. Think about the meaning of each **bold** term. Then, check the Student Dictionary.

Common Nouns	Proper Nouns
mother	Mom
religion	Judaism
building	the White House
city	Paris
month	July

Pretend that you are a teacher. Complete the dialogue with helpful answers.

Student: A noun describes a person, a place, or a thing. Is that right?

Teacher: _____

Student: How can I tell if a noun should be capitalized?

Teacher: _____

Student: But, how do I know if it is a proper noun?

Teacher: _____

Student: I think I get it. But, I'm writing about a particular dog—mine. Should I write *poodle* with a capital *p*?

Teacher: _____

Student: Her name is Missy, short for Mischief. *Missy* and *Mischief* are both proper nouns, right?

Teacher: _____

⭐ Challenge!

Take turns reading the dialogue with a partner. What changes should you make to it? Show your edits above.

Compare Words

Read the paragraph. Think about the meaning of each **bold** word. Then, check the Student Dictionary.

> Is it *exciting*, *wonderful*, or *horrible*? Words that describe a person, a place, or a thing are called **adjectives**. How do you run? Words such as *quickly*, *slowly*, and *fast* are **adverbs**. Adverbs usually describe verbs but might also describe adjectives or other adverbs.

Complete the web to show your understanding of the words *adjective* and *adverb*.

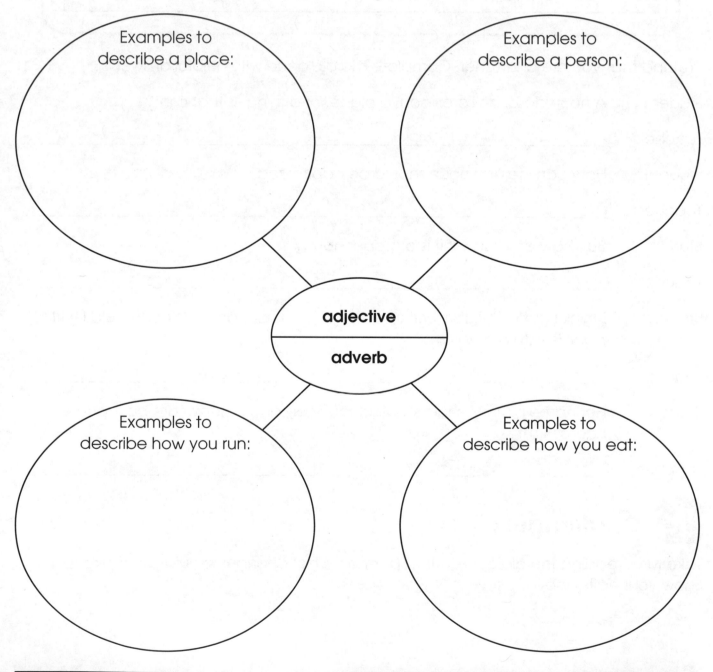

Examples to describe a place:

Examples to describe a person:

adjective

adverb

Examples to describe how you run:

Examples to describe how you eat:

Academic Vocabulary Practice • Grade 3 • CD-104808

Compare Words

Read the chart. Think about the meaning of each bold **word**. Then, check the Student Dictionary.

Facts	Opinions
Pennsylvania is a state. Winter begins in December. Dogs are mammals.	Pennsylvania is beautiful! I do not like winter sports. Dogs are the best pets.

Write *facts* or *opinions* to complete the paragraph.

   Statements that can be proven true are (1.) _____. You

can check (2.) _____ by looking in books. You cannot check

(3.) _____. They are what people think or feel. You can agree or

disagree with (4.) _____ but not with (5.) _____.

Think of a sport or an animal. Write a fact about it. Then, write an opinion.

   6. fact: _____

   7. opinion: _____

Make Connections

Read the paragraph. Think about the meaning of each **bold** term. Then, check the Student Dictionary.

> When you read the **dialogue** in a story, how can you tell which **character** is speaking? Look for the words before and after the **quotation marks**. The words inside of the quotation marks are spoken by a character.

Read the dialogue. Then, answer the questions.

"Tonight, we're eating a special treat," announced Mama Mouse.

"Pizza!" cried Andy Mouse.

Allie Mouse said, "No, it must be strawberry cupcakes."

"I'm afraid you're both mistaken," said Mama Mouse. "But, you'll soon see. Just follow me."

---

1. Which characters are speaking the dialogue?

   _____

2. What does Andy Mouse say? How does he sound?

   _____

3. Who says the words *Just follow me*? How can you tell?

   _____

Write dialogue for the next part of the story. Give each character something to say. Use quotation marks correctly.

Mama Mouse led the two children along the wall to the dark kitchen.

_____

_____

_____

Make Connections

Read the paragraph. Think about the meaning of each **bold** term. Then, check the Student Dictionary.

> When you are reading and come to a word you do not know, what should you do? Try looking for a **context clue** before or after the word. You might even find a **definition** of the word. If you cannot find context clues, then use a dictionary to look up the definition.

Read each sentence. Write a short meaning for the underlined word. Circle the term that tells how you found the meaning.

1. The teacher frowns at <u>unruly</u> behavior.

   _____   context clue   definition

2. Dress very warmly on <u>frigid</u> days.

   _____   context clue   definition

3. Some <u>botanists</u>, or plant scientists, study corn.

   _____   context clue   definition

4. <u>Clippers</u> were the fastest sailing ships of their time.

   _____   context clue   definition

5. "Ugh!" said Celia, making a face. "I <u>detest</u> worms."

   _____   context clue   definition

 **Word Alert!**

The three words below are in the same word family. They have related meanings. Try to use at least two of the words in a sentence.

> definition   define   definite

Make Connections

Read the paragraph. Think about the meaning of each **bold** word. Then, check the Student Dictionary.

> The chapters of **fiction** books and **nonfiction** books are listed in the table of contents at the front. Some nonfiction books have an **index** at the back. The listings in an index help readers find the pages that have particular facts. Some books have an extra section of information at the back. This may be called an **appendix**. An appendix may include a **glossary**, which lists and defines some words in the book.

Circle *Yes* or *No* for each question. Write your reason on the line.

1. Is fiction made up by an author?   Yes   No

   _____

2. Are the listings in an index arranged by chapter?   Yes   No

   _____

3. Could a book about butterflies be nonfiction?   Yes   No

   _____

4. Is nonfiction usually not true?   Yes   No

   _____

5. Should the words in a glossary be in alphabetical order? Yes   No

   _____

6. Would a picture book about a talking rat have an index?   Yes   No

   _____

7. Is an appendix more likely to be found in a nonfiction book? Yes   No

   _____

! Word Alert!

The prefix *non-* means "not." How does knowing that help you remember the meaning of *nonfiction*?

_____

Make Connections

Look at the pictures and read the captions. Think about the meaning of each **bold** term. Then, check the Student Dictionary.

biography   pourquoi tale   fantasy   journal

Underline the correct ending to each sentence.

1. A biography is
    A.   a fiction story about someone.
    B.   a nonfiction story about someone.

2. You know you are reading a fantasy when
    A.   impossible things happen.
    B.   characters speak dialogue.

3. The author of a journal writes
    A.   articles for magazines and newspapers.
    B.   facts and opinions about experiences.

4. The French word *pourquoi* means "why." The stories called *pourquoi* tales tell why
    A.   something in nature came to be.
    B.   animal characters act like people.

5. You could read a biography about
    A.   a music star.
    B.   dinosaurs.

Make Connections

Read the tips. Think about the meaning of each **bold** word. Then, check the Student Dictionary.

Tips for Getting Your Story Ready to **Publish**

- Use a list or other plan to write your **draft**.

- As you **edit** or **revise** your draft, pay attention to **sequence**. Make sure you are using helpful words such as *first*, *next*, and *later that day*.

- Do not forget to consider your **audience**.

- As you **proofread**, look for **homophones**. It is easy to confuse *their*, *there*, and *they're*. Make sure you have spelled the words you mean.

Complete each sentence with a vocabulary word.

1. Look for correct use of capital letters when you _____.

2. A first try at putting ideas into writing is called a _____.

3. The order in which things happen is the _____ of events.

4. Write so that your _____ will enjoy and understand your story.

5. When you _____ your writing, you share a final version with readers.

6. When you _____ or _____ your story, you make it better.

7. The words *right*, *write*, and *rite*, are _____.

 **Look It Up!**

The word *draft* has more than one meaning. Use a classroom dictionary to find three definitions. On another sheet of paper, draw three pictures to show the three definitions of *draft*.

Play with Words

Code Words

Choose the word or words that complete each sentence. Circle the letter.

1. Use ___ to figure out word meanings.
   r context clues
   s haiku
   t verbs

2. A word meaning is a ___.
   e definition
   f journal
   g plural

3. The words *school* and *student* are ___.
   u verbs
   v nouns
   w homophones

4. The word *replay* has a ___.
   g nonfiction
   h suffix
   i prefix

5. A noun that names one thing is ___.
   s singular
   t synonym
   u plural

6. A ___ is a kind of fiction.
   c fact
   d homophone
   e fantasy

Write the circled letters in order. You will find the answer to this question: *What is good advice for any writer?*

_____!

Play with Words

Hidden Message

Read each clue. Find and circle the vocabulary word that matches the clue.

1. *read* and *reed*   h o h o m o p h o n e s w i s

2. first, next, after that, last   t h e l e s e q u e n c e t t

3. *icy* and *frozen*   e r k l i s y n o n y m s k e f

4. the *-ly* in *gladly*   l o u r y o s u f f i x u c a

5. more than one   n t m a k e c a p l u r a l k e w

6. antonym for *fact*   i t h o o p i n i o n u t i t

Look back to find the letters you did NOT circle. Write them in order on the lines to find a riddle and its answer.

___ ___ ___   ___ ___   ___ ___ ___   ___ ___ ___ ___ ___

___   ___ ___ ___ ___   ___ ___ ___ ___ ___?

___ ___ ___   ___ ___

___ ___ ___ ___   ___ ___ ___ ___ ___ ___   ___ ___!

Important Social Studies Words You Need to Know

Use this list to keep track of how well you know the new words.

0 = Don't Know   1 = Know Somewhat   2 = Know Well

___ ancient

___ archaeology

___ architecture

___ century

___ civilization

___ colonist

___ culture

___ custom

___ decade

___ ethnic

___ explorer

___ festival

___ folktale

___ human rights

___ Independence Day

___ Labor Day

___ Memorial Day

___ millennium

___ monument

___ myth

___ native

___ settlement

___ symbol

Explore a Word

Name _____

Read the paragraph. Think about the meaning of the **bold** term.

> People want their leaders to treat them fairly. Fair treatment is a basic part of **human rights**.

1. What do you think the term means? Write your idea.

   human rights: _____

   _____

2. Write a sentence with the term **human rights**. Show what it means.

   _____

   _____

3. Check the meaning of **human rights** in the Student Dictionary.

4. If your sentence in step 2 matches the meaning, put a ✓ after it. If your sentence does not match the meaning, write a better sentence.

   _____

   _____

5. Make a simple drawing to show the meaning of **human rights**.

Academic Vocabulary Practice • Grade 3 • CD-104808

Compare Words

Read the paragraph. Think about the meaning of each **bold** word. Then, check the Student Dictionary.

> People have always built **monuments** to heroes, events, and ideas. For example, the Washington Monument in Washington, DC, honors George Washington. The Statue of Liberty in New York Harbor is a **symbol** of welcome.

Think of a person from the past or a past event that you think deserves a monument. Draw the monument. Then, complete the sentences.

1. This monument is called _____ .

2. It is made of _____ .

3. The monument honors _____ .

4. When people visit this monument, they will _____

   _____ .

5. This monument is a symbol of _____ .

Compare Words

Read the sentence. Think about the meaning of each **bold** word. Then, check the Student Dictionary.

> The first **decade** of the twentieth **century** lasted from 1900 to 1909. A **millennium** is a period of 1,000 years.

Circle the word that completes each sentence.

1. A (century/decade) lasts 100 years.

2. We live in the twenty-first (century/decade).

3. A 10-year-old has lived for a (century/decade).

4. A world war took place during the (century/decade) of the 1940s.

5. Laura's great grandfather has lived for a (century/decade).

6. The year 2000 was celebrated as the beginning of another (decade/millennium).

 ## Look It Up!

Use a classroom dictionary to find words that begin with *cent-*. List three words that have to do with 100 parts or things. Tell a partner what each one ha-s to do with the meaning "100."

_____

_____

_____

Compare Words

Read the paragraph. Think about the meaning of each **bold** term. Then, check the Student Dictionary.

> Every year, on the last Monday in May, Americans observe **Memorial Day**. Every year on July 4, Americans celebrate **Independence Day**. The first Monday in September is **Labor Day**, a special holiday to celebrate all working people.

Read each sentence. Does it tell about Memorial Day, Independence Day, or Labor Day? Circle the answer.

1. In 1776, a group of men met in Philadelphia. They signed a document declaring that they wanted to be free of Great Britain.

   Memorial Day   Independence Day   Labor Day

2. Americans gather to remember people in the armed forces who gave their lives for their country.

   Memorial Day   Independence Day   Labor Day

3. A day was set aside to honor all workers who contribute to the prosperity and well-being of the United States.

   Memorial Day   Independence Day   Labor Day

4. Crowds cheer and clap as fireworks explode in the night sky.

   Memorial Day   Independence Day   Labor Day

5. Flowers and flags are placed on graves.

   Memorial Day   Independence Day   Labor Day

! Word Alert!

Memorial begins with *mem-*, a root that has to do with thinking back on the past. Other words with that root are *memory* and *remember*. Read the sentence. Underline the word with the root *mem*. Tell what you think it means.

   A holiday is a way to commemorate an important event.

_____

Make Connections

Read the paragraph. Think about the meaning of each **bold** word. Then, check the Student Dictionary.

> **Explorers** from Europe first arrived in North and South America in the late 1400s. They found **native** people living in small and large **settlements**. In the 1500s, European **colonists** began arriving to start their own settlements.

Complete each sentence with a vocabulary word.

1. The country where you were born is your _____ land.

2. Christopher Columbus and Francisco Pizarro were _____ who claimed land for Spain.

3. The earliest _____ from England lived in Virginia and Massachusetts.

4. The Dutch built a _____ on land that is now New York City.

5. _____ made the first maps of rivers and lakes in North America.

❗ Word Alert!

A suffix is a word part added to the end of a word. The suffixes *-ist* and *-er* can name people. Complete each sentence with a word related to the underlined word.

6. People who live in a <u>colony</u> are called _____.

7. People who <u>explore</u> are called _____.

8. People who _____ are called <u>settlers</u>.

Make Connections

Read the paragraph. Think about the meaning of each **bold** word. Then, check the Student Dictionary.

> Do you like to eat Chinese food? What about Italian food? China and Italy have given the world different foods. These are sometimes called **ethnic** foods. Ways of cooking and eating are part of a people's **culture**. Other parts of a culture are **customs** such as religious practices and **festivals**. A culture also includes stories such as **folktales** and **myths**.

Circle *Yes* or *No* for each question. Write your reason on the line.

1. Is a festival usually a quiet time?   Yes   No

   _____

2. Is storytelling part of a group's culture?   Yes   No

   _____

3. Is a myth like a true adventure story?   Yes   No

   _____

4. Does a folktale come from the "folk" of the past?   Yes   No

   _____

5. Do people today have customs?   Yes   No

   _____

6. Do you like to eat ethnic food?   Yes   No

   _____

Make Connections

Read the sentence. Think about the meaning of each **bold** word. Then, check the Student Dictionary.

> Because of **archaeology**, we now know about the art, **architecture**, beliefs, and rulers of the **civilization** of the **ancient** Maya in Mexico and Central America.

Underline the correct ending to each sentence.

1. If you studied archaeology, you would learn
    A. how to build skyscrapers.
    B. how to dig up objects buried long ago.

2. An ancient culture is
    A. very old.
    B. religious.

3. Signs of an ancient civilization are
    A. paintings in caves.
    B. half-buried buildings of a city.

4. You can see examples of architecture
    A. in the buildings around you.
    B. in styles of clothing.

5. Words that could describe any civilization are
    A. *ancient* and *important*.
    B. *large* and *organized*.

⭐ Challenge!

Reread the sentence at the top of the page. Write two or three sentences to explain what the sentence means. Do not use any of the vocabulary words in your explanation.

_____

_____

_____

Play with Words

Letter by Letter

Choose the word that fits with each clue. Write it letter by letter. Some letters will be inside circles.

ancient	colonist	customs	decade
explorer	folktale	rights	

1. Opposite of modern Ⓞ _ _ _ _ _ _

2. Weddings, festivals, manners _ _ Ⓞ _ _ _ _

3. Synonym for searcher _ Ⓞ _ _ _ _ _ _

4. An old story Ⓞ _ _ _ _ _ _ _

5. A settler from another land _ _ _ _ Ⓞ _ _ _

6. Human ___ _ _ Ⓞ _ _ _

7. 10 years _ Ⓞ _ _ _ _

Write the circled letters in order. You will find the answer to this riddle: *What is full of holes yet still holds water?*

_ _   _ _ _ _ _ _

Play with Words

Code Words

Choose the word or words that complete each sentence. Circle the letter.

1. The Fourth of July is also called ___.
   g a monument
   h Independence Day
   i Memorial Day

2. The ___ had a few houses.
   a settlement
   b festival
   c archaeology

3. Remember American soldiers on ___.
   p Memorial Day
   q historians
   r architecture

4. Freedom of speech and religion are ___.
   n native customs
   o ancient cultures
   p human rights

5. A museum of ___ shows ancient objects.
   c monuments
   d architecture
   e archaeology

6. The ___ of ancient Rome lasted for centuries.
   m archaeology
   n civilization
   o decades

Write the circled letters in order on the line. You will complete a question that a historian asks.

What really did _____?

Academic Vocabulary Practice • Grade 3 • CD-104808

Important Geography Words You Need to Know

Use this list to keep track of how well you know the new words.

0 = Don't Know   1 = Know Somewhat   2 = Know Well

___ capital

___ cliff

___ climate

___ coastal

___ continent

___ county

___ desert

___ elevation

___ environment

___ equator

___ grassland

___ harbor

___ hemisphere

___ island

___ kilometer

___ landform

___ local

___ mesa

___ mountain pass

___ North America

___ North Pole

___ peninsula

___ plain

___ port

___ scale

___ South Pole

___ tide

___ valley

___ weather

Explore a Word

Read the sentence. Think about the meaning of the **bold** word.

> People and other living things need an **environment** with clean water.

1. What do you think the word means? Write your idea.

   environment: _____

   _____

2. Write a sentence with the word **environment**. Show what it means.

   _____

   _____

3. Check the meaning of **environment** in the Student Dictionary.

4. If your sentence in step 2 matches the meaning, put a ✓ after it. If your sentence does not match the meaning, write a better sentence.

   _____

   _____

5. Make a simple drawing to show the meaning of **environment**.

Academic Vocabulary Practice • Grade 3 • CD-104808

Compare Words

Read the sentence. Think about the meaning of each **bold** word. Then, check the Student Dictionary.

> Our **climate** has cold **weather** for several months each year.

Read each sentence. Does it tell about climate or weather? Circle the answer.

I.	Dark clouds mean it is going to rain.	climate	weather
2.	Rain falls almost every day of the year.	climate	weather
3.	All year, days are hot, and nights are cool.	climate	weather
4.	There is a wet season and a dry season.	climate	weather
5.	The sky is sunny and bright today.	climate	weather
6.	Plants grow all year.	climate	weather
7.	Strong winds blew down trees.	climate	weather
8.	A big snowstorm buried roads.	climate	weather

Answer the question with your own idea.

9. What is the weather like in the climate where you live?

_____

_____

Compare Words

Look at the pictures and read the captions. Think about the meaning of each **bold** word. Then, check the Student Dictionary.

| desert | grassland |

Circle the word in parentheses that completes each sentence.

1. Some (deserts, grasslands) are in climates that have a rainy season.

2. The plants of a (desert, grassland) can live without much water.

3. Some (deserts, grasslands) have huge hills of sand.

4. Many natural (deserts, grasslands) have been turned into farms.

5. A (desert, grassland) may be hot or cold, but it is always dry.

6. Many animals live underground in a hot (desert, grassland) because there is little shade to keep them cool.

! Word Alert!

Two words put together are called a compound word. One of the vocabulary words is a compound word. Write a meaning for it. Include both of the smaller words in your meaning.

_____

Academic Vocabulary Practice • Grade 3 • CD-104808

Make Connections

Look at the picture and read the caption. Think about the meaning of each **bold** word. Then, check the Student Dictionary.

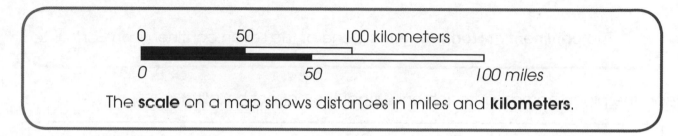

The **scale** on a map shows distances in miles and **kilometers**.

Underline the correct ending to each sentence.

1. Mapmakers use a scale to show
   A. that miles and kilometers are both measures of distance.
   B. how real-world distances compare to lengths on the map.

2. A distance of 50 kilometers might be shown on a map as
   A. 2 inches.
   B. 30 miles.

3. An example of a scale is
   A. 1 inch equals 10 miles.
   B. 1 kilometer equals 1,000 meters.

4. Use a scale to measure the distance
   A. in kilometer-miles.
   B. in miles or in kilometers.

5. A kilometer is
   A. shorter than a mile.
   B. longer than a mile.

 **Look It Up!**

Look up the word *scale* in a classroom dictionary. You will find separately numbered entries. Use three of the definitions to complete the sentences.

1. Use a balance scale to _____ .

2. Use a scale of distance to _____ .

3. The scales on a fish _____ .

Make Connections

Read the sentence. Think about the meaning of each **bold** term. Then, check the Student Dictionary.

> The **continent** of **North America** is one of the seven continents on Earth.

Read the place names. List each one under the correct heading.

Canada	Europe	Australia
Asia	Antarctica	Central America
Greenland	Mexico	South America
North America	Caribbean Islands	Africa
United States		

Names of Continents	Places in North America

Make Connections

Read the paragraph. Think about the meaning of each **bold** term. Then, check the Student Dictionary.

> People who live north or south of the **equator** have a summer of long days and a winter of short days. People who live at the equator, however, have days and nights of equal length all year long. The equator divides the planet into the Northern and Southern **Hemispheres**. The **North Pole** is located at the very top of the Northern Hemisphere. The **South Pole** is located at the very bottom of the Southern Hemisphere. Sunlight is experienced in extremes at the poles. There may be 24 hours of sunlight or 24 hours of darkness at certain times of the year.

Complete each sentence with a vocabulary word.

1. Earth is divided into two hemispheres by the _____.

2. The half of Earth that lies below the equator is the _____ Hemisphere.

3. The half of Earth that lies above the equator is the _____ Hemisphere.

4. The farthest point south of the equator is the _____ _____.

5. The farthest point north of the equator is the _____ _____.

6. Make a simple drawing of a globe. Draw lines and points if necessary and label them using the vocabulary words.

Make Connections

Read the paragraph. Think about the meaning of each **bold** word. Then, check the Student Dictionary.

> The government of a state or a country is based in a city called the **capital**. A **county** is an area with **local** government. A town or a city called the county seat is the center of the county's government.

Underline the correct ending to each sentence.

1. A county is part of a
   A. city.
   B. state.

2. The capital of the United States is
   A. Washington, DC
   B. the state of Washington.

3. A local event could take place
   A. throughout a country.
   B. in a neighborhood.

4. The state of Texas has many
   A. counties.
   B. capitals.

5. A leader of a local government is
   A. a mayor.
   B. a US senator.

 Challenge!

Could a capital city be a county seat? Write a reason for your answer.

_____

_____

Make Connections

Read the paragraph. Think about the meaning of each **bold** term. Then, check the Student Dictionary.

> The travelers climbed from the **valley** up eastern slopes that became steeper and steeper. At last, they reached the **mountain pass** that led to the other side. At the high **elevation**, they could see the western forests far below.

Circle *Yes* or *No* for each question. Write your reason on the line.

1. Is land at sea level at a high elevation?　　　　　　　　　　Yes　　No

_____

2. Is a valley always next to a mountain?　　　　　　　　　　Yes　　No

_____

3. Is a mountain pass like a passage?　　　　　　　　　　　Yes　　No

_____

4. Could people live in a valley?　　　　　　　　　　　　　Yes　　No

_____

❗ Word Alert!

The words *elevator* and *elevation* are in the same word family. They have related meanings. Another word in the same family is underlined in the sentence below. Write a meaning for that word. Use what you know about the meanings of *elevator* and *elevation*.

We rode on an <u>elevated</u> train.

_____

_____

Make Connections

Read the paragraph. Think about the meaning of each **bold** word. Then, check the Student Dictionary.

> Valleys, mountains, hills . . . how many **landforms** can you name? A **plain** is flat land with few trees. A **mesa** is also flat, but it is higher than the land below and has steep sides. A **cliff** is also high and steep. If you stand on the edge of a cliff, you will probably see water far below. A **peninsula** is a piece of land that juts out into water on three sides. An **island** is a tract of land that is surrounded by water on all sides.

Complete each sentence with a vocabulary word.

1. Waves splash against the base of the _____.

2. Drive on a highway in the southwestern United States, and you may see a _____ rising in the distance.

3. Cliffs, mesas, and plains are examples of _____.

4. Much of the US state of Florida is a _____.

5. A mesa is like a _____, because both are high landforms.

6. A plain is like a _____, because both have flat surfaces.

7. People can become stranded on an _____ in a large lake or the ocean.

 ## Word Alert!

Homophones are words that sound alike but have different spellings and meanings. One of the vocabulary words is a homophone for *plane*. Write the vocabulary word on the blank to complete the sentence. Then, tell what the sentence means in your own words.

The plane flew over the _____.

_____

_____

Make Connections

Read the paragraph. Think about the meaning of each **bold** word. Then, check the Student Dictionary.

> Some people in **coastal** areas depend on fishing. The level of water in a **harbor** rises and falls with the **tides**, so the best time to set sail may be at high tide. Fishing boats return to the **port** to unload their catches.

Underline the correct ending to each sentence.

1. A coastal region is never
    A. inland.
    B. an island.

2. A harbor could be
    A. deep or shallow.
    B. a river or a stream.

3. If you were on a beach at low tide, you would
    A. see few or no waves reach the shore.
    B. walk farther to reach the water's edge.

4. Coastal cities have ports where
    A. trading ships dock.
    B. airplanes land.

5. A harbor is like a
    A. port.
    B. tide.

6. You can tell from the names of the cities Portland, Portsmouth, and Greenport that the cities are
    A. by water.
    B. in cold climates.

Play with Words

Code Words

Choose the word or words that complete each sentence. Circle the letter.

1. The ___ of Canada is Ottawa.
    c continent
    d capital
    e North America

2. A map is drawn to a ___.
    e scale
    f climate
    g landform

3. An area of low land is a ___.
    q cliff
    r tide
    s valley

4. A city might grow near a good ___.
    l kilometer
    m county
    e harbor

5. A ___ is a high, flat landform.
    r mesa
    s plain
    t mountain pass

6. North America is ___.
    s an environment
    t a continent
    u a natural resource

Write the circled letters in order. You will find the name of a type of land in a dry climate.

_____

 Academic Vocabulary Practice • Grade 3 • CD-104808

Play with Words

Vocabulary Crossword Puzzle

Use the clues to solve the crossword puzzle.

ACROSS
1   South America
4   Cold, windy, rainy _____
5   By the seashore
6   1,000 meters
7   A large, flat landform

DOWN
2   Distance above sea level
3   A low land
5   Corn, wheat, oranges

Important Civics and Economics Words You Need to Know

Use this list to keep track of how well you know the new words.

0 = Don't Know   1 = Know Somewhat   2 = Know Well

___ authority

___ barter

___ budget

___ citizenship

___ civic responsibility

___ civil rights

___ common good

___ consumer

___ currency

___ direct democracy

___ duty

___ economy

___ exchange

___ expense

___ export

___ federal

___ illegal

___ import

___ income

___ industry

___ legal

___ legislature

___ manufacturing

___ mayor

___ office

___ producer

___ profit

___ public service

___ represent

___ representative democracy

___ tolerance

Academic Vocabulary Practice • Grade 3 • CD-104808

Explore a Word

Read the sentences. Think about the meaning of the **bold** word. Then, check the Student Dictionary.

> One person's beliefs may be the opposite of another person's beliefs. But, the two people can get along if they show **tolerance**.
>
> Americans are free to practice any religion they choose. A government shows religious tolerance by not interfering with people's choices.

Fill in the web to show your ideas about tolerance.

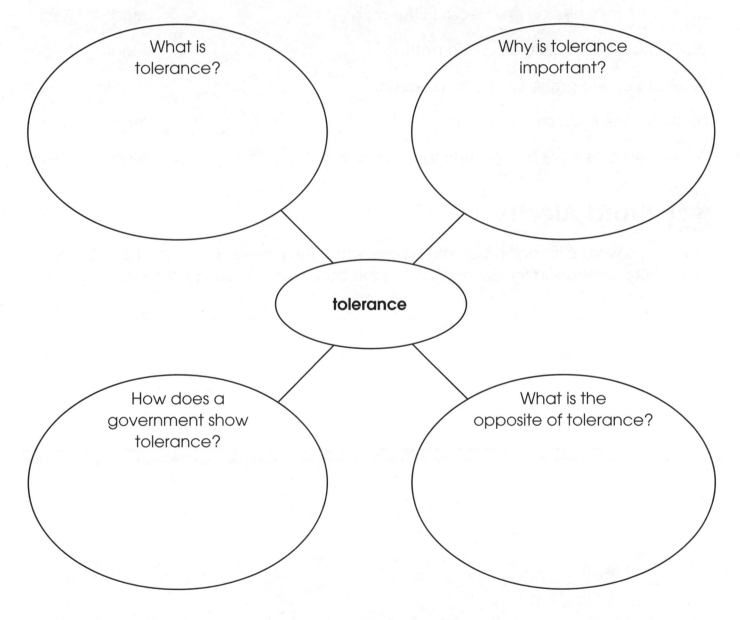

What is tolerance?

Why is tolerance important?

tolerance

How does a government show tolerance?

What is the opposite of tolerance?

Compare Words

Read the sentences. Think about the meaning of each **bold** word. Then, check the Student Dictionary.

> It is **legal** to cross a street at a crosswalk. It is **illegal** to drop litter on a sidewalk.

Read each sentence. Is the action legal or illegal? Circle the answer.

1. Myra unbuckles her seat belt in a moving car.   legal   illegal

2. Matt keeps his dog on a leash in the park.   legal   illegal

3. Sasha rides her bike on a bike path.   legal   illegal

4. A big crowd gathers to hear a speech.   legal   illegal

5. A gas line leaks oil into a river.   legal   illegal

6. A child pulls a fire alarm when there is no fire.   legal   illegal

 Word Alert!

A prefix is a word part added before a base word. The prefixes *il-*, *im-*, and *in-* can mean "not." Write a meaning for each word. Use the base word in your meaning.

1. illegal: _____

2. imperfect: _____

3. incomplete: _____

Compare Words

Read the paragraph. Think about the meaning of each **bold** word. Then, check the Student Dictionary.

> US farmers grow soybeans that other countries want to buy. Soybeans are a major US **export**. The United States does not grow much coffee, so it **imports** coffee from other countries.

Circle the word in parentheses that completes each sentence.

1. An (import/export) is a product that comes into a country and is sent by the country where it was made.

2. Farmers grow crops that are (imported/exported) to foreign lands.

3. A country must (import/export) oil if it does not have enough oil of its own.

4. Factories might buy (imported/exported) metals to use in making new products.

5. China makes and (imports/exports) more products to the United States than the United States sells to China.

 **Challenge!**

Imports and exports have to do with the balance of trade between two countries. What do you think *balance of trade* means? Draw a picture to show its meaning. Use the words *imports* and *exports* in your drawing.

Compare Words

Read the paragraph. Think about the meaning of each **bold** word. Then, check the Student Dictionary.

> When was the last time you were a **consumer**? It might have been today, if you spent any money. Anyone who buys a product is a consumer. A consumer also buys services such as a haircut or a car wash. The businesses that make products or provide services are called **producers**.

Follow each instruction.

1. Name two producers who provide services.

   _____

2. Name two things that factories produce.

   _____

3. Circle the word that is a synonym for *consumer* in the sentence.

   The customer purchased a box of fruit.

4. Complete the sentence below with your own idea.

   Producers want consumers to _____

   _____ .

5. Explain what the sentence means in your own words.

   At times, a producer is also a consumer.

   _____

   _____

Make Connections

Read the paragraph. Think about the meaning of each **bold** word. Then, check the Student Dictionary.

> The US president is elected to **office** for a four-year term. The president has the **authority** to name people who will hold other offices such as the secretary of defense or the secretary of education.

Complete each sentence with your own idea.

1. A school has an office. But, that kind of office is different from the kind of office that someone holds. The difference is _____

   _____ .

2. Students do not have the authority to change school rules. The people with that authority are _____

   _____ .

3. Voters elect a leader to a government office. They give that person the authority to _____

   _____ .

4. Citizens may want to meet with someone who holds an office of authority in government. The reason for the meeting might be _____

   _____ .

 **Word Alert!**

Read the sentence to find three words from the same word family. Write the three words on the line.

The governor's office gave official orders to the officers of the state police.

_____

_____

Make Connections

Read the paragraph. Think about the meaning of each **bold** word. Then, check the Student Dictionary.

> A person, a family, and a government all earn **income**. Their **budgets** show how they will use the income to pay for the things they need and other **expenses**.

Underline the correct ending to each sentence.

1. Most people get their income from
    A. their jobs.
    B. their travels.

2. A government gets its income from
    A. taxes.
    B. producers.

3. A family's budget must include
    A. the cost of food.
    B. the selling of services.

4. A budget helps a person
    A. keep track of spending.
    B. earn more money at work.

5. If someone does not have enough money to buy something right now, a budget can help the person
    A. use a credit card to borrow money.
    B. set aside some income as savings.

6. An item likely to be listed in a person's budget is
    A. clothing.
    B. friendship.

Make Connections

Read the paragraph. Think about the meaning of each **bold** term. Then, check the Student Dictionary.

> "Thank you for electing me," said the **mayor** to the people of the city. "I have worked in **public service** my whole life. And, I intend to keep working for the **common good**."

Use your ideas to complete each sentence with one or more words that make sense.

1. City _____ are a public service that people use for transportation.

2. Workers who provide public services include teachers, firefighters, and _____.

3. The common good _____ all members of a group.

4. A government _____ for the common good.

5. A public service such as _____ is provided for the common good.

6. Taxpayers _____ the public services that everyone uses.

7. The _____ of a city is the head of its government.

8. Mayors work in _____ for the good of the people who live in their cities.

Make Connections

Read the paragraph. Think about the meaning of each **bold** word. Then, check the Student Dictionary.

> Businesses in every **industry** try to make a **profit**. For example, the **manufacturing** of sneakers costs money. To make a profit, the factory owners must sell their sneakers for more money than they paid to make them.

Underline the correct ending to each sentence.

1. An example of an industry is
    A.   making a profit.
    B.   building houses.

2. Most manufacturing takes place in
    A.   factories.
    B.   schools.

3. To make a profit, a business must
    A.   spend more than it earns.
    B.   earn more than it spends.

4. Examples of manufactured products are
    A.   stoves and sinks.
    B.   fire and water.

5. Fishing, mining, and transportation are all
    A.   industries.
    B.   manufacturers.

6. If a toy store does not make a profit,
    A.   toy manufacturing will grow.
    B.   the store might have to close.

Make Connections

Read the paragraph. Think about the meaning of each **bold** word. Then, check the Student Dictionary.

> Imagine an **economy** in which there was no such thing as money. In an economy based on **barter**, a farmer might barter vegetables for cloth woven by a traveling weaver. The invention of **currency** meant that the farmer could **exchange** vegetables for coins or paper money. Then, the farmer could use the money to buy cloth and other products.

Complete each sentence with a vocabulary word from the paragraph above.

1. The US dollar is a kind of _____.

2. A growing _____ means more jobs and more profits for businesses.

3. A big problem with _____ is that someone with a product that you want might not be willing to trade with you.

4. The _____ of goods and services is part of every economy.

5. Japanese units of currency are called *yen*. Americans traveling in Japan would _____ US dollars for yen.

 # Look It Up!

How can you find the names of currencies used throughout the world? A dictionary lists each name. Some dictionaries also give a table of currencies with the entry *currency*. Play a dictionary game with a partner to match a currency to its country or countries. Here are some currencies to start with: *yen, euro, pound, peso, ruble, rupee,* and *dinar*.

Make Connections

Read the paragraph. Think about the meaning of each **bold** term. Then, check the Student Dictionary.

> Citizens want a government that respects their **civil rights**. **Citizenship** brings rights, but it also brings **duties**. Citizens show **civic responsibility** in many ways. One important way is by voting. Civic responsibilities also include obeying laws and staying informed about government matters.

Circle *Yes* or *No* for each question. Write your reason on the line.

1. Are civil rights like human rights?   Yes   No

   _____

2. Do students your age have any duties?   Yes   No

   _____

3. Is paying taxes a civic responsibility?   Yes   No

   _____

4. Do civil rights have to do with war?   Yes   No

   _____

5. Are Americans the only people with citizenship?   Yes   No

   _____

Make Connections

Read the paragraph. Think about the meaning of each **bold** term. Then, check the Student Dictionary.

> The United States has a **federal** system of government. Each state in the union gives certain powers to the central government. The US government is also a **representative democracy**. Voters elect members of the **legislature** to **represent** citizens' interests. A representative democracy is different from a **direct democracy**, in which the citizens vote on laws themselves.

Complete each sentence with your own idea.

1. In a representative democracy, citizens do not govern themselves directly. Instead, they _____

   _____ .

2. A state has its own government. But, the federal government can tell _____

   _____

   _____ .

3. The members of a legislature try to decide _____

   _____ .

4. Voters choose a person to represent them. The voters believe that the person will

   _____

   _____ .

5. A direct democracy is not a good system for governing millions of people. There would be problems because _____

   _____ .

Play with Words

Code Words

Choose the word or words that complete each sentence. Circle the letter.

1. Trash collection is ___.
   p a public service
   q a civil right
   r an import

2. The members of a legislature ___ citizens.
   q exchange
   r represent
   s export

3. Trading a service for goods is ___.
   n illegal
   o barter
   p industry

4. A dollar is a unit of ___.
   d budget
   e economy
   f currency

5. ___ produces goods.
   h A consumer
   i Manufacturing
   j An import

6. ___ includes goods and services.
   t An economy
   b Citizenship
   c Civic responsibility

Write the circled letters in order. You will find a word that answers this question: *What is a business owner's goal?*

_____

Play with Words

Hidden Message

Read each clue. Find and circle the vocabulary word that matches the clue.

1. Respect for others' views

   t h t o l e r a n c e e m o r

2. A user of a product

   e y o u t c o n s u m e r a k

3. ___ rights

   e f r o c i v i l m i t t h e b

4. US voters have this.

   i g g e c i t i z e n s h i p r i t

5. Lawful

   g e t s w h l e g a l a t i s

6. The US Congress

   i t a h l e g i s l a t u r e o l e

Look back to find the letters you did NOT circle. Write them in order to find a riddle and its answer.

___ ___   ___ ___ ___ ___   ___ ___ ___   ___ ___ ___ ___

___ ___ ___ ___   ___ ___,   ___ ___ ___   ___ ___ ___ ___ ___ ___

___ ___   ___ ___ ___ ___ ___.   ___ ___ ___ ___   ___ ___   ___ ___?

(___   ___ ___ ___ ___)

Important Art
Words You Need to Know

Use this list to keep track of how well you know the new words.

0 = Don't Know   1 = Know Somewhat   2 = Know Well

___ animation

___ ballet

___ chord

___ chorus

___ cityscape

___ concert

___ cool colors

___ duet

___ horizontal

___ landscape

___ melody

___ performance

___ position

___ quartet

___ seascape

___ still life

___ tempo

___ trio

___ vertical

___ warm color

Explore a Word

Read the sentence. Think about the meaning of the bold word.

> Artists use computers to make **animations** that look like real-life movements.

1. What do you think the word means? Write your idea.

    animation:_____

    _____

2. Write a sentence with the word **animation**. Show what it means.

    _____

    _____

3. Check the meaning of **animation** in the Student Dictionary.

4. If your sentence in step 2 matches the meaning, place a ✓ after it. If your sentence does not match the meaning, write a better sentence.

    _____

    _____

5. Make a simple drawing to show the meaning of **animation**.

Explore a Word

Read the sentence. Think about the meaning of the **bold** word. Then, check the Student Dictionary.

> The audience cheered and clapped during the dance **performance**.

Fill in the web to show your ideas about performances.

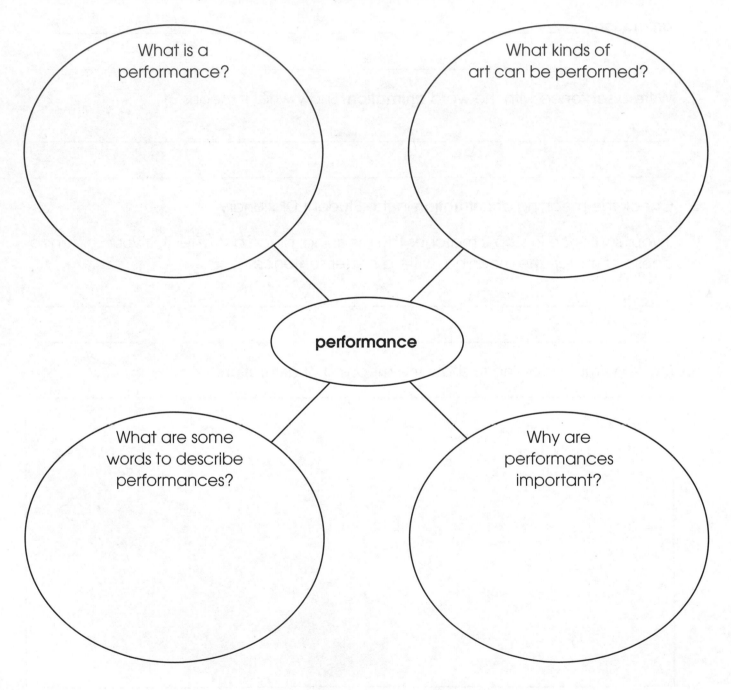

Compare Words

Read the paragraph. Think about the meaning of each **bold** word. Then, check the Student Dictionary.

> Hold your arms out to your sides as far as they will stretch. The imaginary line between your hands is **horizontal**. Picture a line from the top of your head to your feet. The imaginary line is **vertical**.

Follow each instruction.

1. Draw an uppercase letter *T* in the box. Write *vertical* and *horizontal* to label the lines in the letter.

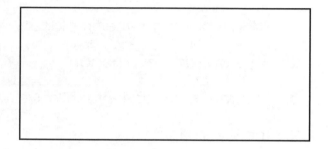

2. Write an uppercase letter that has one vertical line and three horizontal lines.

   _____

3. Name two horizontal shapes you see around you.

   _____

4. Name two vertical shapes you see around you.

   _____

5. Draw a pattern of horizontal and vertical lines. Make it interesting by varying the thickness of the lines and the size of the spaces.

 Look It Up!

Look up *horizon* in a classroom dictionary. Draw or write to show how it is related in meaning to *horizontal*.

_____

_____

Compare Words

Read the paragraph. Think about the meaning of each **bold** term. Then, check the Student Dictionary.

> The artist used **cool colors** to show water and **warm colors** to show the setting sun. The water is blue green, and the sky is pink orange.

Read each sentence. Does it tell about a warm color or a cool color? Circle the answer.

1. A log is burning in the fireplace.	warm color	cool color
2. A yellow sun is overhead.	warm color	cool color
3. The trees have dark-green leaves.	warm color	cool color
4. The sky is bright blue.	warm color	cool color
5. Blue-purple plums fill the bowl.	warm color	cool color
6. The glass is filled with orange juice.	warm color	cool color
7. Red tulips grow against a fence.	warm color	cool color
8. Green ferns grow by a stream.	warm color	cool color

Make Connections

Read the sentence. Think about the meaning of each **bold** word. Then, check the Student Dictionary.

> Children begin their study of **ballet** by learning the five basic **positions** of the feet.

Use your ideas to complete each sentence with one or more words that make sense.

1. In any form of dance, the positions of the _____ and feet are important.

2. Special shoes help a ballet dancer _____ on the tips of her toes.

3. Ballet dancers train hard to make _____ and spins look easy.

4. A ballet dancer is able to position _____ so that the foot points to the ceiling.

5. Ballet dancers change their positions as they listen _____.

★ Challenge!

The word *ballet* comes from France, because France was home to schools of ballet long ago. To this day, ballet terms are in French. Find a person who has studied ballet. Ask for three ballet terms. Then, use a dictionary to try to find the spellings of those terms.

Make Connections

Read the paragraph. Think about the meaning of each **bold** word. Then, check the Student Dictionary.

> A **trio** of musicians played a song. A fourth musician joined in, and the **quartet** played together. Then, a man and a woman came onstage to sing a **duet**.

Underline the correct ending to each sentence.

1. A duet may be performed by
   A.   two musicians.
   B.   three singers.

2. A singing trio has
   A.   exactly three singers.
   B.   at least three singers.

3. A quartet could include
   A.   two singers and four musicians.
   B.   two violins, a viola, and a cello.

4. The singers of a duet
   A.   perform alone and together.
   B.   must be a male and a female.

5. The difference between a trio and a quartet is that
   A.   a trio has one more performer.
   B.   a quartet has one more performer.

 ## Word Alert!

One of the vocabulary words has the number prefix *tri-*. Read the words. Underline the prefix *tri-* in each. Then, tell how all of the words are alike in meaning.

> triangle   tricycle   trio   triple   triplet

Make Connections

Read the paragraph. Think about the meaning of each **bold** term. Then, check the Student Dictionary.

> Some paintings and drawings are **still lifes**. In a still life, an artist shows objects that are not moving. A still life is usually set indoors. Outdoor scenes are shown in **landscapes** or **seascapes** of the natural world. A **cityscape** shows streets and buildings.

Read the title of each painting. Imagine what the painting looks like. Write the vocabulary word that names the kind of painting.

1. *Three Lemons in a Glass Bowl* _____

2. *Ocean Bay at Sunset* _____

3. *Green Buses on Silver Bridge* _____

4. *Forest Waterfall* _____

5. *View from Rocky Hill* _____

 **Challenge!**

Choose one of the paintings from above. Make a sketch to show what you would include in a painting with that title. Use another sheet of paper if necessary.

Make Connections

Read the paragraph. Think about the meaning of each **bold** word. Then, check the Student Dictionary.

> The teacher played a few **chords** on the piano. Then, she played a **melody** while the **chorus** sang along. The song began at a slow **tempo** but became faster and livelier. The chorus is getting ready for a **concert** for students, teachers, and parents.

Circle *Yes* or *No* for each question. Write your reason on the line.

1. Can a chorus have just one person?   Yes   No

    _____

2. Could someone hum a chord?   Yes   No

    _____

3. Is a melody the same as a note?   Yes   No

    _____

4. Does a tempo have to do with speed?   Yes   No

    _____

5. Is a concert like a performance?   Yes   No

    _____

Play with Words

Code Words

Choose the word that completes each sentence. Circle the letter.

1. Several notes played at once make a ___.
   a melody
   b chord
   c chorus

2. A drawing of an outdoor scene could be a ___.
   c vertical
   d still life
   e cityscape

3. Light blue is a ___.
   a cool color
   b warm color
   c tempo

4. A tune is also called a ___.
   s chord
   t duet
   u melody

5. The ocean meets the sky in a ___ line.
   t horizontal
   u vertical
   v seascape

6. A painting of books on a table is a ___.
   w performance
   x position
   y still life

Write the circled letters in order. You will find a word that answers this question: *What do artists often think about?*

_____

Play with Words

Vocabulary Crossword Puzzle

Use the clues to solve the crossword puzzle.

ACROSS

2   A group of singers
5   From top to bottom
6   First ___ in ballet
8   A cartoon

DOWN

1   A synonym for concert
3   A painting of water
4   Red and orange are ___ colors.
7   Duet, ___, quartet

Game Ideas and Suggestions

Use games and activities to help students better hear, see, and remember content-area vocabulary words. The suggestions on these pages can be used with the words in this book and with any other vocabulary words that students are learning.

Charades

Choose about 10 vocabulary words. Write the words on slips of paper and display them. Give students time to think about the words before removing the slips. Then, divide the class into two teams. One team member chooses a slip, holds up fingers to indicate the number of syllables, and pantomimes the word. Teammates try to guess the word within a certain time limit.

Word Art

Help students select vocabulary words to depict as art. Encourage them to use letter shapes and arrangements to indicate what the words mean. Prompt students with questions such as "How might you arrange the letters of the word *valley*?", or "What might happen to the letters in *evaporate*?"

Vocabulary Word-O!

Reproduce the Word-O! game card on page 107 and distribute to each student. Write 20 vocabulary words on slips of paper and display the slips. Have students choose nine words to write on their cards. Shuffle the slips and then choose one slip at a time. Instead of reading the word aloud, offer a clue about it. For example, for the word *numerator*, you might start with the content area: "This is a math word that has to do with fractions." Or, use a strong context sentence with "blank" for the word: "In the fraction three-fourths, three is the 'blank.'" Students should check off the word if it is on their grids. The first student to complete three across, down, or diagonally says "Word-O!" and reads aloud the three words.

Connect a Word

Have students name a vocabulary word for you to write on the board. Draw a box around the word. Then, randomly choose another vocabulary word and write it in a box to the right of the first word. Have individual students or partners take turns trying to make a sentence that contains both words. If the group agrees that the sentence makes sense (even if it is silly), draw an arrow between the boxes to connect them. To make the game more challenging, use vocabulary words from different content areas.

Card Pairs

Use index cards cut in half to prepare a deck of 52 cards. Write 26 vocabulary words and 26 synonyms or short definitions on the cards. The cards can be used in a variety of games such as Memory or Concentration. Below is one suggestion.

- **Go Fish!** for 2 to 5 Players
- Each player is dealt five cards. The remaining cards are placed facedown in a pile.

Game Ideas and Suggestions

- The player to the right of the dealer starts by setting aside any pairs. Then, she asks the player on the right for a card needed to make a pair. "Do you have *antonym*?", or "Do you have the meaning of *antonym*?"

- If the holder has the requested card, he hands it over. If the holder does not have it, the player must "go fish" and draw the top card from the pile. If no match can be made, the next player takes a turn.

- The winner is the first player with no cards in hand or the player with the most pairs after all cards have been drawn.

Word Hunt

Emphasize that vocabulary words appear in print and online in a variety of informational resources. As you come across a vocabulary word—in a headline, a news article, an advertisement, or another resource—save the printed source or make a printout. Challenge students to read the text to find the vocabulary word and to explain what it means in the provided context.

Dictionary Guess

Have one student randomly choose a word from the Student Dictionary and read the definition aloud to the class. Partners or small groups then try to write the vocabulary word that matches the definition. Continue until each student has had a chance to choose a word and read its definition aloud. Award a point for each correct word.

Racetrack Games

Have students design their own racetrack board games or make one from a template you provide, such as the template on page 108. Here is one way to use the template:

- Select 20 vocabulary words for students to write in the spaces.

- Make a small cardboard spinner by drawing a circle divided into three sections labeled 1, 2, and 3. The "spinner" can be a paper clip attached to a paper fastener.

- Provide small objects for students to use as markers.

- Each player spins, and the player with the highest number goes first.

- The player spins and moves the marker the number of spaces shown. The player must say the word on the space and demonstrate knowledge of it by giving its definition or using it in a good context sentence.

- Players may use a dictionary to check the player's response. A player who is not correct loses a turn.

- The first player to reach the finish line wins.

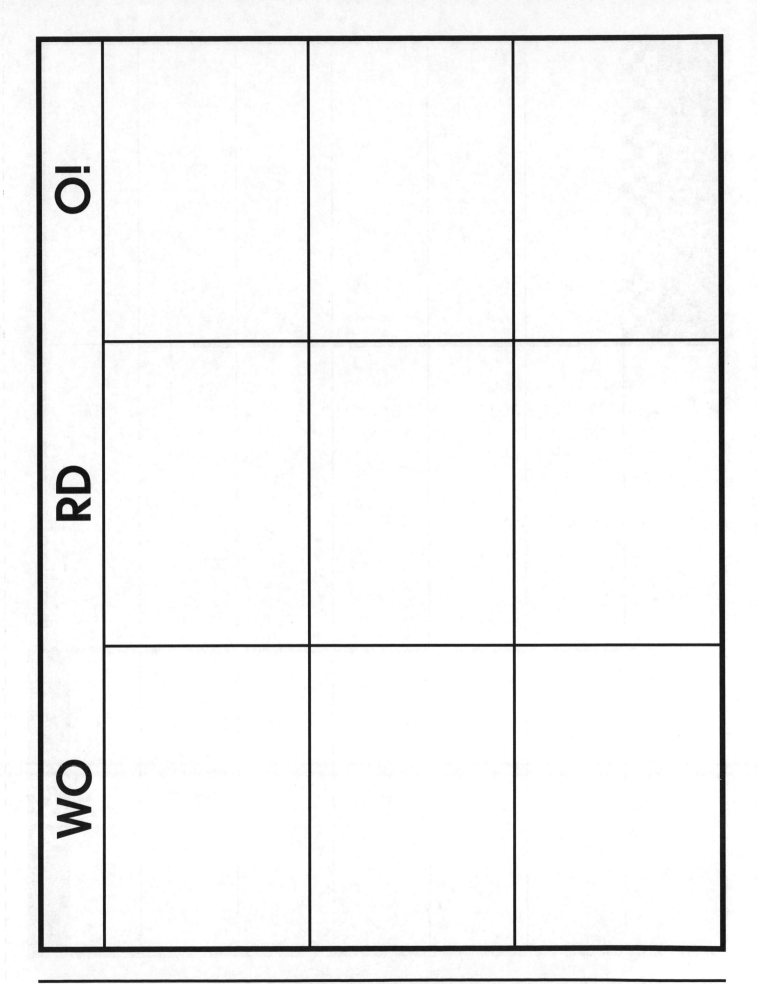

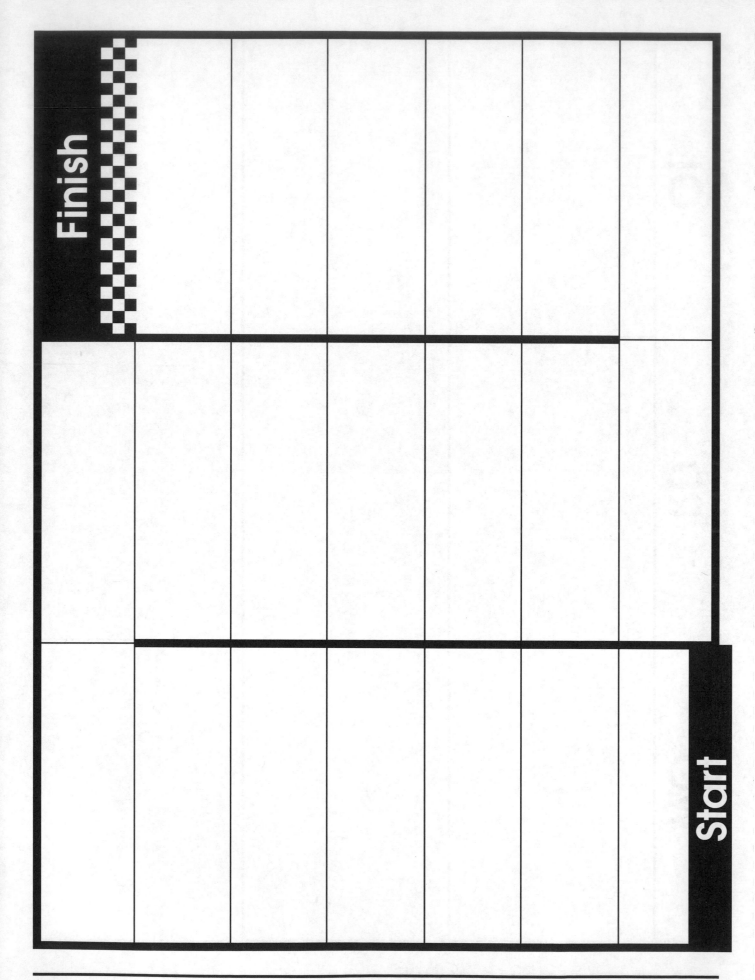

Academic Vocabulary Practice • Grade 3 • CD-104808

Student Dictionary

Important Math Words I Need to Know

algorithm (AL gah ri thim) *noun* A step-by-step way of solving a problem that always works.

angle (AN gul) *noun* The space between two lines that meet at an endpoint, or the space between two flat surfaces that meet at a line.

area (AIR ee uh) *noun* The number of square units that fill a surface. *The bedroom has an area of 120 square feet.*

bar graph (bar graf) *noun phrase* A type of graph that uses rectangular bars of different heights, or lengths, to show and compare different amounts.

capacity (ka PA se tee) *noun* The ability to hold or contain something.

decimal point (DES ih mul point) *noun phrase* The dot in a number that separates whole numbers from tenths, hundredths, thousandths, and so on. A decimal point separates dollars from cents in written amounts of money.

denominator (dih NOM ih nay ter) *noun* The number below the line in a fraction. The denominator tells how many equal parts the whole has been broken into.

diagonal (dy AG nul) *noun* A slanted line that connects opposite corners.

digit (DIJ it) *noun* One of the numbers 0 to 9.

dividend (DI va dend) *noun* The number that is divided in a division problem.

divisor (di VI zer) *noun* The number by which a number is being divided.

division (dih VIZH un) *noun* Figuring out how many times one amount can fit into another amount; the act of dividing. *We used division to split 45 crayons evenly among three friends.*

equilateral triangle (EE kwuh lat ur ul TRY an gul) or (EK wuh lat er ul) *noun phrase* A triangle with three sides of equal length.

equivalent (e KWIV a lent) *adjective* Having the same value.

estimate (ES ta mat) *verb* To roughly judge the value, size, or cost of something.

factor (FAK ter) *noun* One of two or more numbers that are multiplied in a multiplication problem.

fraction (FRAK shun) *noun* A part of a whole. *Add the fractions $\frac{1}{2}$ and $\frac{1}{2}$ to get 1.*

hexagon (HEK suh gon) *noun* A flat shape with six sides. A hexagon may have six sides of equal or different lengths.

line segment (lin SEG ment) *noun phrase* A line linking two points

measurement (MEZH ur mint) *noun* The use of standard units to tell length, size, weight, amount, time, and so on. *Meter sticks, tablespoons, and balance scales are three tools used for measurement.*

multiple (MUL tuh pul) *noun* A number that can be divided evenly by a particular number. *The number 3 has the multiples 6, 9, 12, 15, and so on.*

multiplication (mul tuh plih KAY shun) *noun* Adding a number to itself two or more times; the act of multiplying. *We used multiplication to figure out how many crayons we needed in order to give 5 crayons to each of 25 children.*

numerator (NOO mur ay tur) *noun* The number above the line in a fraction. The numerator tells how many parts of the whole are noted.

octagon (OK tuh gon) *noun* A flat shape with eight sides. An octagon may have eight sides of equal or different lengths.

parallel (PER a lel) *adjective* Being an equal distance apart everywhere and never touching.

pentagon (PEN tuh gon) *noun* A flat shape with five sides. A pentagon may have five sides of equal or different lengths.

Academic Vocabulary Practice • Grade 3 • CD-104808

Important Math Words I Need to Know

perimeter (puh RIM uh tur) *noun* The distance around the outside of a flat shape.

perpendicular (pur pin DIK yuh lur) *adjective* Describing two lines that cross at right angles, one going left and right, and the other going up and down. *The top edge and the side edge of a sheet of paper are perpendicular.*

pictograph (PIK ta graf) *noun* A graph that uscs pictures or symbols to represent data.

polygon (POL ee gon) *noun* A flat shape formed by three or more line segments. Triangles, squares, and octagons are examples of polygons.

product (PROD ukt) *noun* The answer in a multiplication problem. *Multiply 10 times 10 to get the product of 100.*

quotient (KWOH shunt) *noun* The answer in a division problem. *Divide 100 by 10 to get the quotient of 10.*

rectangle (REK tang gul) *noun* A flat shape with four sides and four right angles. *A square is a rectangle with four equal sides.*

remainder (rih MAYN dur) *noun* The number left over when a number is not divided evenly. *If two friends divide 9 candies, each friend will have 4 candies, and there will be a remainder of 1.*

right triangle (rite TRY an gul) *noun phrase* A triangle with two sides that meet to form a right angle. A right angle is 90 degrees and is formed by two perpendicular lines.

tally chart (TA lee chart) *noun phrase* A table that uses tally marks to show how many times a value appears.

volume (VOL yum) *noun* The amount of space occupied by a three-dimensional object.

Vocabulary Notes

_____

_____

_____

_____

_____

_____

_____

_____

_____

Important Science Words I Need to Know

adaptation (ad ap TAY shun) *noun* A body part or a behavior that allows a life form to live in an environment. *Webbed feet are an adaptation that helps ducks swim.*

asteroid (AS tuh roid) *noun* A rock that is in orbit around the sun. An asteroid is smaller than a planet.

astronomer (uh STRON uh mur) *noun* A scientist who studies space and the bodies in it.

axis (AK sis) *noun* An imaginary line that cuts through a planet. The planet spins around the line. *Earth spins on an axis through the North and South Poles.*

carnivore (KAR nih vor) *noun* **1.** An animal that eats other animals. **2.** A member of a group of meat-eating mammals that includes dogs, cats, and bears.

comet (KOM it) *noun* An icy body in space that has a long tail of gas and dust. In the solar system, comets take a long orbit around the sun. *Halley's Comet can be seen as it nears the sun about every 76 years.*

condense (kun DENS) *verb* To change from a gas into a liquid. *Drops of water condense on a bathroom mirror after you take a hot shower.*

decomposer (dee kum POH zur) *noun* A life form that breaks down the remains of dead plants and animals into simple nutrients that return to the soil to nourish plants. Most decomposers are bacteria and fungi.

ecosystem (EK oh sis tim) *noun* A community of living things along with the nonliving things in a natural area. *Scientists study how the sun's energy flows from plants to other living things in an ecosystem.*

evaporate (ih VAP uh rayt) *verb* To change from a liquid to a gas. *As the air heated, the puddles on the street evaporated.*

food web (FOOD WEB) *noun phrase* The network of connections among plants, animals that eat plants, and animals that eat plant-eaters. Diagrams of food webs have arrows showing how energy flows from the things that are eaten to the eaters.

gas (gas) *noun* A state of matter without a definite shape. The tiniest particles, or atoms, of the gas spread out to fill any space. *People breathe out the gas called carbon dioxide.*

habitat (HAB ih tat) *noun* The natural area in which a plant or an animal lives. *A stream is a habitat for beavers.*

herbivore (HER bih vor) *noun* An animal that feeds mainly on plants.

humidity (hyoo MID ih tee) *noun* The amount of moisture in the air. *Summer days with high humidity feel steamy.*

liquid (LIH kwid) *noun* A state of matter that changes shape and takes up a definite amount of space. The tiniest particles of the matter, or its atoms, are arranged more loosely than in a solid but more tightly than in a gas.

matter (MAT ur) *noun* Anything that can be weighed and takes up space.

nutrient (NOO tree int) *noun* A substance that nourishes, or feeds, living things. *Water and proteins are basic nutrients for humans.*

overheat (oh vur HEET) *verb* To become too hot.

orbit (OR bit) *noun* The path that a planet or other body takes around a star, or the path that a moon takes around its planet. *verb* To take a path around a body in space.

omnivore (OM ni vor) *noun* An animal that eats both plants and other animals.

overheated (o ver HE ted) *adjective* Too hot.

perspire (pur SPIRE) *verb* To get rid of water through small holes, or pores, in the skin; to sweat.

Important Science Words I Need to Know

plasma (PLAZ ma) *noun* Gas that has been ionized or energized.

precipitation (prih sip ih TAY shun) *noun* A form of water that falls to Earth's surface. Rain, hail, snow, and sleet are precipitation.

predator (PRED uh tur) *noun* An animal that hunts and eats other animals.

prey (pray) *noun* Animals that are hunted and eaten by other animals. *Rabbits must be alert and fast to avoid becoming prey.*

producer (pruh DOO sur) *noun* A life form that uses the sun's energy and nonliving substances to make its own food. Green plants are producers that other living things depend on.

reproduce (REE pruh doos) *verb* To make more living things of the same kind. *Birds reproduce by making eggs.*

revolve (rih VOLV) *verb* To take a circular path around a central object. *Planets revolve around the sun.*

rotate (ROH tayt) *verb* To turn like a wheel around a central point or line.

solar system (SOH lur SIS tim) *noun phrase* The sun and all of the bodies that revolve around it. Planets, their moons, and comets are some of the bodies in our solar system.

solid (SOL id) *noun* A state of matter that has a definite shape and takes up a certain amount of space. The tiniest particles of the matter, or its atoms, are arranged more tightly in a solid than in a liquid or a gas.

species (SPEE sheez) *noun* A grouping of life forms in which all of the members look like one another and can produce offspring together. *Scientists are still naming new species of plants and insects.*

tilt (tilt) *verb* To slant. *Earth tilts to one side as it travels around the sun.*

water cycle (WAH tur SY kul]) *noun phrase* The never-ending changes that water goes through as it moves throughout Earth. Water evaporates from bodies of water, rises into the sky as a gas, and then condenses to a liquid to fall back to the surface.

water vapor (WAH tur VAY per) *noun phrase* Water in the form of a gas.

Vocabulary Notes

_____

_____

_____

_____

_____

_____

_____

Important Technology Words I Need to Know

brainstorm (BRAYN storm) *verb* To think of ideas to solve problems, usually by talking in a group.

browser (BROU zur) *noun* A computer program that locates and shows information from the Internet and other networks.

engineer (EN jin eer) *noun* A person who uses science to design, plan, and build machines, buildings, products, and other technologies.

gear (geer) *noun* A simple machine made of at least two toothed wheels that turn together. The wheels may be connected directly or with a belt that moves between them.

home page (hom paj) *noun phrase* The main page on a website that is seen first and usually contains links to other parts of the site.

Internet (IN tur net) *noun* The worldwide network that connects computer networks. The Internet connects a computer to email, the World Wide Web, and other services.

inventor (in VENT er) *noun* A person who creates or produces something for the first time.

pulley (PUL ee) *noun* A simple machine that is made of a wheel with a grooved rim for a rope or a belt. Pulling on one end of the rope lifts an object on the other end.

ramp (ramp) *noun* A slope or inclined plane that joins two surfaces that are at different levels or heights.

recycle (ree SY kul) *verb* To take out useful materials from things that are thrown away and find new uses for those materials. *We fill bins with paper and plastic so that they will be recycled into new products.*

reduce (rih DOOS) *verb* To lower the amount of something. *We reduced our use of paper by writing on both sides of every sheet.*

reuse (ree YOOZ) *verb* To use again. *Instead of throwing out paper bags, we reuse them as book covers.*

simple machine (SIM pul muh SHEEN) *noun phrase* One of the six basic machines that are used alone or as part of other machines to make work easier. Simple machines have no or few moving parts. The six simple machines are the ramp, pulley, wheel and axle, gear, wedge, lever, and screw.

surf (serf) *verb* To search for information on the Internet.

technology (tek NO la jee) *noun* The use of science, especially in industry and engineering, to invent useful things or to solve problems.

website (WEB site) *noun* A place on the World Wide Web that contains information about a person, organization, etc.

wheel and axle (WEEL and AK sul) *noun phrase* A simple machine that is made of a rod, called an axle, attached to the center of a wheel. Turning the axle causes the wheel to turn. Or, turning the wheel causes the axle to turn.

Important Language Arts Words I Need to Know

adjective (AJ ik tiv) *noun* A word that describes a noun. *Examples:* <u>round</u>, <u>sweet</u>, <u>hard</u> *candy*.

adverb (AD verb) *noun* A word that describes a verb, adjective, or another adverb.

antonym (AN tuh nim) *noun* A word with an opposite meaning. *The words* hot *and* cold *are antonyms.*

appendix (a PEN diks) *noun* A section or a table of extra information added at the end of a book.

audience (AU de en(t)s) *noun* The people reading a text, listening to a speaker, or watching a performance.

biography (by OG ruh fee) *noun* The true story of a person's life.

character (KER ik ter) *noun* A person who appears in a book, a story, a play, a movie, or a TV show.

common noun (KAH men naun) *noun phrase* A word or a group of words that name a person, a place, or a thing.

context clue (KON tekst kloo) *noun phrase* An idea in the words around an unknown word, which point to the meaning of the unknown word.

definition (def ih NIH shun) *noun* The meaning of a word.

dialogue (DY uh log) *noun* The words spoken by characters in a story.

draft (draeft) *noun* An early form of a written work. *verb* To write the first form of a work.

edit (EH dit) *verb* To prepare something written to be published by making changes, correcting mistakes, etc.

fact (fakt) *noun* A piece of information that is true and can be proved.

fantasy (FAN tuh see) *noun* A fiction story in which things happen that could never happen in real life. *The children flew to the moon on the back of a winged horse in this fantasy.*

fiction (FiK shun) *noun* A story that is made up by the author.

glossary (GLOS sa ree) *noun* An alphabetical list that gives definitions of words in a book.

haiku (HY koo) *noun* A three-line poem with a syllable pattern of 5-7-5 and no rhyme. The poem is usually about nature. Haiku are based on a Japanese form of poetry.

homophone (HOM uh fone) *noun* A word that sounds like another word but has a different spelling and meaning. *The words* rain, rein, *and* reign *are homophones.*

index (IN deks) *noun* A part of a book that lists topics in the book and gives the pages where information can be found. An index is usually in the back of the book. *The index to the book about dinosaurs lists 10 pages of information about their eating habits.*

journal (JUR nul) *noun* A daily record of experiences and thoughts. *Some writers share their journals, but others keep them private.*

nonfiction (non FiK shun) *noun* A true story or other written work that gives information. Nonfiction is about things that really happened and does not come from the author's imagination. Science books, history books, and biographies are examples of nonfiction.

noun (naun) *noun* A word that names a person, a place, or a thing. *Examples: mother, country, book.*

opinion (uh PIN yun) *noun* An idea that a person believes. An opinion cannot be proved true, and others may disagree with it. *Sandra's opinion is that it is more fun to play tennis than basketball.*

plural (PLUR ul) *noun, adjective* A noun that names more than one person, place, or thing. Most plurals are formed by adding the ending -s or -es. *Examples of plural nouns: foxes, clouds, kittens, teeth.*

Important Language Arts Words I Need to Know

pourquoi tale (por KWAH tayl) *noun phrase* An old story that tells how something in nature came to be. *We read a pourquoi tale about how the elephant got its trunk.*

prefix (PREE fiks) *noun* A word part added before a word to change its meaning. *Examples: retell, undo, nonfiction.*

proofread (PROOF reed) *verb* To read a final copy of a written work carefully to find and fix mistakes in spelling, capital letters, punctuation, and so on.

proper noun (PRO per 'naun) *noun phrase* A word or a group of words that name a particular person, place, or thing and usually begin with a capital letter.

publish (PUB lish) *verb* To share a final, correct copy of a written work with readers.

quotation marks (KWOH tay shun marks) *noun phrase* The punctuation marks (" ") used with dialogue that show where a speaker's exact words begin and end.

revise (rih VIZE) *verb* To make changes to the draft of a written work. *Some writers revise their stories dozens of times to make the stories better and better.*

sequence (SEE kwins) *noun* The order in which things happen. *Give the sequence of events in the story by telling what happens in the beginning, the middle, and the end.*

singular (SING gyuh lur) *adjective* Of a noun that names just one person, place, or thing. *Examples of singular nouns: fox, cloud, kitten, tooth.*

suffix (SUF iks) *noun* A word part added after a word to change its meaning or change the way it is used in a sentence. *Examples: pester, loudly, careful.*

synonym (SIN uh nim) *noun* A word with a similar meaning. *The words* small *and* little *are synonyms.*

verb (vuhrb) *noun* A word that shows action or shows what something is. *Examples: Birds fly. Insects buzz. The cat naps. We are happy.*

Vocabulary Notes

Academic Vocabulary Practice • Grade 3 • CD-104808

Important Social Studies Words I Need to Know

ancient (AYN shunt) *adjective* Of the long-ago past.

archaeology (ar kee OL uh jee) *noun* The study of human ways of life long ago. The methods of archaeology involve careful digging in areas where people once lived.

architecture (AR kih tek chur) *noun* **1.** The designing of buildings. **2.** The buildings of a particular time or place. *The architecture of modern cities includes tall glass buildings.*

century (SEN chur ee) *noun* A period of 100 years. *The eighteenth century began in the year 1700.*

civilization (siv il ih ZAY shun) *noun* An organized society of people who build cities, have a political system, and develop the arts. *Sculpture was an advanced art during the civilization of ancient Greece.*

colonist (KOL uh nist) *noun* A person living in a land governed by a faraway country.

culture (KUL chur) *noun* The beliefs, customs, and arts of a people. *Pop music is a part of American culture.*

custom (KUS tum) *noun* A way of behaving that is shared by the members of a nation or a group. *The customs of Vietnam include showing respect to elders.*

decade (DEK ayd) *noun* A period of 10 years.

ethnic (ETH nik) *adjective* Pertaining to races or large groups of people who share the same customs, religions, origin, etc.

explorer (ik SPLOR ur) *noun* A person who travels through an area to learn about it.

festival (FES tuh vul) *noun* A time for celebrating and feasting, often linked to an important event.

folktale (FOHK tayl) *noun* A story without an author, first told long ago and passed down through the years. *"Jack and the Beanstalk" is a folktale.*

human rights (HYOO mun rites) *plural noun phrase* The basic freedoms that belong to all people. Human rights in the US and many other countries include the right to live where and how one wishes, the right to a fair trial, the right to worship as one wishes, and the right to speak one's opinions.

Independence Day (in duh PEN dins day) *noun* The US holiday held July 4 to celebrate the signing of the Declaration of Independence in 1776.

Labor Day (LA ber day) *noun phrase* A holiday celebrated in the United States on the first Monday in September to honor working people.

Memorial Day (muh MOR ee ul day) *noun phrase* The US holiday, observed on the last Monday in May, to honor the members of the armed forces who gave their lives in service to their country.

millennium (ma LE ne um) *noun* A period of 1,000 years.

monument (MON yuh mint) *noun* A building, statue, or other structure erected to remember an important person, event, or idea.

myth (mith) *noun* An ancient story that tells about gods, goddesses, heroes, and magical events. *The Greek god Zeus plays a role in many myths.*

native (NAY tiv) *adjective* **1.** Of the first people to live in an area. *American Indians were natives living in America when the Europeans arrived.* **2.** Of the land of one's birth.

settlement (SET ul mint) *noun* **1.** A place in which people new to an area have built homes. **2.** A small group of people living together.

symbol (SIM ball) *noun* Something that stands for something else.

Important Geography Words I Need to Know

capital (KAP ih tul) *noun* A city that is the center of government of a state or a country.

cliff (klif) *noun* A high, steep, rocky slope that usually overlooks a large body of water.

climate (KLY mit) *noun* The temperatures, rainfall, and other weather conditions that a region usually has. *The climate near the North Pole includes long, harsh winters and short, cool summers.*

coastal (KOH stul) *adjective* Of or near the seashore.

continent (KON tih nint) *noun* One of the seven large land masses on Earth's surface.

county (KOUN tee) *noun* An area within a state that has its own government for certain activities. *The county jail is run by a sheriff.*

desert (DEZ urt) *noun* A land that gets little rainfall.

elevation (el uh VAY shun) *noun* The height above sea level.

environment (in VY urn mint) *noun* The natural area in which plants, animals, and people live.

equator (e KWA ter) *noun* An imaginary line that divides Earth into two parts, the Southern Hemisphere and the Northern Hemisphere.

grassland (GRAS land) *noun* A land that gets enough rainfall to grow short or tall grasses. Some trees grow in a grassland, but most of the plants are low to the ground.

harbor (HAR bur) *noun* The part of a body of water that is near land, where ships stay when they are not at sea.

hemisphere (HEM eh sfeer) *noun* One of the two halves of Earth, below or above the equator.

island (I land) *noun* A piece of land that is surrounded by water.

kilometer (KIL uh mee tur) or (kil OM ih tur) *noun* A measure of distance equal to 1,000 meters and about six-tenths of a mile.

landform *noun* A natural feature on Earth's surface, such as a mountain, a valley, or a canyon.

local (LO kul) *adjective* Having to do with activities that are near a known place such as a home neighborhood.

mesa (MAY suh) *noun* A high area of land with steep sides. The word *mesa* is Spanish for "table" because mesas look like tabletops.

mountain pass (MOUN tun pas) *noun phrase* A narrow gap between mountains that allows travel from one side of a mountain range to the other.

North America (north uh MEH rih kuh) *noun phrase* One of the seven continents on Earth. North America includes Canada, the United States, Mexico, Central America, the islands of the Caribbean Sea, and the island of Greenland in the northern Atlantic Ocean.

North Pole (north pol) *noun phrase* The northernmost point on Earth.

peninsula (pe NIN(t) s(a) la) *noun* A piece of land that juts out and is surrounded by water on three sides.

plain (playn) *noun* A large area of mainly flat land with few trees. A vast area of central North America is called the Great Plains.

port (port) *noun* **1.** A place on a body of water where ships can load and unload their goods. **2.** A safe place for ships to wait; a harbor.

scale (skayl) *noun* A measuring tool on a map that shows inches or centimeters standing for distances on Earth's surface. *The scale of distance on the map shows that one inch stands for a distance of 100 miles.*

Academic Vocabulary Practice • Grade 3 • CD-104808

Important Geography Words I Need to Know

South Pole (sauth pol) *noun phrase* The southernmost point on Earth.

tide *noun* The daily rise and fall of ocean waters. A high tide and a low tide occur about every 12 hours.

valley (VAL ee) *noun* A long, low area of land. Rivers often run through valleys.

weather (WETH ur) *noun* Temperature, clouds, wind, rain, and other conditions related to the layers of air above Earth's surface in a particular place and time.

Vocabulary Notes

_____

_____

_____

_____

_____

_____

_____

_____

_____

_____

_____

_____

_____

_____

Important Civics and Economics Words I Need to Know

authority (uh THO rih ti) *noun* The right to make decisions and give commands.

barter (BAR tur) *noun* To make a direct trade of products or services.

budget (BUJ it) *noun* A plan that shows how money will be spent over a certain time period. *verb* To make a budget.

citizenship (SIT ih zin ship) *noun* **1.** The state of being a citizen of a country. **2.** The responsibilities of a citizen.

civic responsibility (SIV ik rih spon suh BIL ih tee) *noun phrase* The duty of a citizen or a member of a community or country. *Keeping a neighborhood safe is a civic responsibility.*

civil rights (SIV il rites) *plural noun phrase* Equal treatment under the law and other rights of citizens.

common good (KOM un good) *noun* The good effects for all when people join to form a community.

consumer (kun SOO mur) *noun* Someone who buys and uses products and services.

currency (KUR un see) *noun* The unit of money used in a country. *Coins and paper bills are forms of currency.*

direct democracy (dih REKT dih MOK ruh see) *noun phrase* A form of self-government in which citizens serve as their own lawmakers.

duty (DOO tee) *noun* An action that someone is supposed to do; a responsibility.

economy (ih KON uh mee) *noun* All of the activities connected to producing and consuming goods and services in a country or other place.

exchange (iks CHAYNJ) *verb* To make a trade.

expense (ik SPEN(T)S) *noun* An amount of money that is paid for goods or services.

export (EKS port) *noun* A product that is made in one country and sent to consumers in another country. *verb* To export products by sending them out of a country.

federal (FED uh rul) *adjective* Of a central government created by states that joined together.

illegal (ih LEE gul) *adjective* Against the law.

import (IM port) *noun* A product that is made in another country and used by consumers in the receiving country. *verb* To import products sent by another country.

income (IN kum) *noun* Money that is received. *People's jobs are their source of income.*

industry (IN duh stree) *noun* The businesses involved in making certain kinds of goods or providing services such as manufacturing or tourism.

legal (LEE gul) *adjective* **1.** Allowed by law. **2.** Having to do with laws and lawmakers.

legislature (LEJ ih slay chur) *noun* The body of lawmakers in the government of a country or state. *The US Congress is the national legislature.*

manufacturing (man yuh FAK chur ing) *noun* The making of products in factories.

mayor (MA yer) *noun* An official elected to be head of a city.

office (OF is) *noun* **1.** A position of responsibility. *A governor holds the highest office in the state.* **2.** A department or an agency of the US government. *The Government Printing Office publishes documents.*

producer (pruh DOO sur) *noun* A person or a business that makes a product or provides a service.

profit (PROF it) *noun* The money that a business has left after paying expenses.

public service (PUB lik SUR vis) *noun* The work of providing the public with health, safety, transportation, education, and other services.

represent (REP rih zent) *noun* To act for others. *Elected lawmakers represent the people from their districts or states.*

Important Civics and Economics Words I Need to Know

representative democracy (rep rih ZENT uh tiv dih MOK ruh see) *noun phrase* A form of self-government in which citizens elect leaders and lawmakers who will take actions for them.

tolerance (TOL uh rens) *noun* Respect for the beliefs and practices of others when they are different from one's own.

Vocabulary Notes

_____

_____

_____

_____

_____

_____

_____

_____

_____

_____

_____

_____

_____

_____

Important Art Words I Need to Know

animation (an ih MAY shun) *noun* The drawing of shapes in a series so that the shapes appear to be moving. *Movies with cartoon characters show the art of animation.*

ballet (ba LAY) *noun* A form of dance with particular positions, steps, leaps, and spins. Women ballet dancers perform many moves on the tips of their toes.

chord (kord) *noun* Two or more musical notes played at the same time.

chorus (KOR us) *noun* A group of people who sing together.

cityscape (SIT ee skayp) *noun* A painting, drawing, or photograph that shows a scene of a city or town.

concert (KON surt) *noun* A musical performance.

cool color (kool KUL ur) *noun phrase* Green, blue, and purple. Cool colors suggest places and things that have cool temperatures.

duet (doo ET) *noun* A song or piece of music for two voices or instruments.

horizontal (hor ih ZON tul) *adjective* Of a line or a shape that goes left and right. *Cross the letter* T *with a horizontal line.*

landscape (LAND skayp) *noun* A painting, a drawing, or a photograph that shows an outdoor scene, usually of nature.

melody (MEL uh dee) *noun* The series of musical notes that work together and have a rhythm. A song or a part of a song that has a melody.

performance (pur FOR muns) *noun* A work of music or dance, a play, or another work of art that is shown to an audience.

position (puh ZISH un) *noun* The way in which something, such as a body part, is placed. *Dancers learn basic positions of the feet.*

quartet (kwor TET) *noun* **1.** A group of four singers or musicians. **2.** A musical piece written for four voices or instruments.

seascape (SEE skayp) *noun* A painting, a drawing, or a photograph that shows a scene of an ocean, a coast, or a lake.

still life (stil laif) *noun phrase* A painting, a drawing, or a photograph of objects arranged in a certain way. Fruit and glass objects are common subjects in still lifes.

tempo (TEM poh) *noun* The speed at which music is performed.

trio (TREE oh) *noun* **1.** A group of three singers or musicians. **2.** A musical piece written for three voices or instruments.

vertical (VUR tih kul) *adjective* Of a line or a shape that goes up and down. *A tall building is a vertical shape.*

warm color (warm KUL ur) *noun phrase* Red, orange, and yellow. Warm colors suggest fire and other warm things.

Academic Vocabulary Practice • Grade 3 • CD-104808

Answer Key

Math

Page 6

1-4. Students use this page to assess their knowledge of *algorithm*. 5. *Solution*: 1. Add 100s (400) ; 2. Add 10s (80) ; 3. Add ones (9); 4. Add partial sums (489).

Page 7

1. perimeter, area; The drawing shows a square with each side 1 mile. 2. perimeter, area; The drawing shows a square with each side 3 feet and 9 squares inside. 3. area, perimeter; The drawing shows a rectangle marked 3 inches by 5 inches and 15 squares inside.

Page 8

1. parallel; 2. perpendicular; 3. diagonal; 4. Diagonal; 5. perpendicular; 6. parallel; 7. diagonal; 8. Answers will vary but may include a chair seat and legs. 9. Answers will vary but may include a slanted bookcase. 10. Answers will vary but may include a window.

Page 9

1-3. Students' graphs will vary but should reflect accurate research and tallies.

Page 10

1. cup; 2. quarts; 3. milliliters; 4. quarts; 5. liters; 6. quarts; 7. cup; 8. cups; 9. liters; 10. milliliters

Page 11

1. 357, 5 circled; 2. $10.52, decimal point circled; 3. Answers will vary but may include: 15.64; 4. They become greater. Answers will vary but may include: In 333, the 3 on the left stands for 300, which is greater than 30 or 3. *Look It Up!* 1. number; 2. finger

Page 12

1. A; 2. A. 3. A. 4. A; 5. B. *Challenge!* Pictures will vary but should show halves and be labeled.

Page 13

1. B; 2. A; 3. B

Page 14

Answers will vary but may include: 1. Yes, a product is the answer to a multiplication problem. 2. No, multiplication is like addition. 3. Yes, $2 \times 6 = 12$. 4. No, $6 \times 6 = 36$. 5. Yes, 3 is a factor of 12. 6. No, it is greater. 7. 6, 12, 18, 24, 30, 36, 42, 48, 54, 60; 8. 1, 2, 3, 4, 5, 6, 10, 12, 15, 20, 30, 60

Page 15

1. $15 \div 3$, $4\overline{)20}$; 2. The division problem is 7 divided by 3 with an answer of 2 r1. It should be labeled with all four vocabulary words. 3. Answers will vary but may include: You have 14 things to put into 3 groups. You can make 4 equal groups of 3, but 2 are left over. *Challenge!* Answers will vary but may include that total is separated into parts, and the quotient tells how many equal parts there are.

Page 16

1. pentagon; 2. octagon; 3. rectangle; 4. hexagon; 5. Yes, a triangle is a polygon because it has 3 connected line segments.

Page 17

1. quotient; 2. hexagon; 3. polygons; 4. multiples; 5. product; 6. fraction; *Answer to message:* You must be an expert!

Page 18

Answers spell *figure*.

Science

Page 20

Answers will vary but may include: *What*: body parts or behaviors that help a living thing survive; *Why*: Plants or animals need them to stay alive; *Plants*: roots that take in water, leaves that take in sunlight; *Animals*: fur for warmth, sharp claws for hunting; *Word Alert!* 1. adaptation; 2. adapt

Page 21

1. carnivores; 2. herbivores; 3. carnivores; 4. herbivores; 5. carnivores; *Challenge!* Answers will vary but may include that herbivores eat plants, carnivores eat meat, and omnivores eat both.

Page 22

1. spider–predator, insects–prey; 2. deer–prey, wolves–predators; 3. robin–predator, earthworm–prey; 4. polar bear–predator, seal–prey; 5. sharks–prey, seals–predators

Page 23

1. A; 2. B; 3. B; 4. A; 5. A; 6. B

Page 24

1. reproduce; 2. habitat; 3. food web; 4. species; 5. reproduce; 6. food web; *Challenge!* Drawings will vary.

Answer Key

Page 25

1. gas; 2. liquid; 3. liquid; 4. plasma; 5. solid; 6. gas; 7. solid; 8. plasma; *Look It Up!* Answers will vary but may include: A matter to discuss is an idea or problem. A state of matter is solid, liquid, or gas.

Page 26

Students should label the whole diagram with *water cycle*, the rising arrows with *evaporate*, the full cloud with *condense*, and the rain with *precipitation*.

Page 27

Answers will vary but may include: 1. water; 2. perspire; 3. sweat forms; 4. holds a lot of; 5. drink water

Page 28

1. orbit; 2. tilts; 3. revolves; 4. axis

Page 29

Answers will vary but may include: 1. No, it is an icy body with an oval orbit. (Or) Yes, it is a body that orbits the sun. 2. No, Earth is part of the solar system. 3. Yes, although the moons also orbit their planets. 4. No, astronomers study space from Earth. 5. No, an asteroid does not orbit a planet. *Look It Up!* astronaut, asterisk, astronomy

Page 30

Answers spell *energy*.

Page 31

ACROSS 5. axis; 6. producers; 7. precipitation; 8. food web; DOWN 1. predators; 2. astronomer; 3. species; 4. ecosystem

Technology

Page 33

Answers will vary but may include: 1. trying to think of as many ideas as you can, usually by talking with others; 2. It is as if there is a high-energy storm in your brain. 3. You are getting ideas from other people, not just yourself. It is a fast kind of thinking. 4. They choose an idea to think about more slowly. 5. Answers will vary.

Page 34

1. inventor; 2. inventor; 3. engineers; 4. engineers; 5. inventors, engineers; *Challenge!* Answers will vary but may include that long ago, an engine was any clever idea for solving problems, and an engineer was the person who thought of it.

Page 35

Answers will vary but may include: 1. use email and go to websites. 2. finds and displays the website with that address. 3. Answers will vary. 4. a colored link, the browser finds and displays a different web page. 5. visit a website made by someone in Africa. 6. (name of browser used in school); *Word Alert!* Internet, interactive, and interconnected are underlined. Answers will vary but may include that computer users linked in networks can play games together. Their screens change depending on their actions.

Page 36

Answers will vary but may include: 1. No, a ramp has no moving parts. 2. No, it has many machines working together. 3. No, it moves a longer distance. 4. Yes, a ladder is shaped like a ramp, and climbing it is easier than climbing straight up. 5. Yes, you have to push it up. *Activity:* Drawings and answers will vary: Pushing an object up or down a ramp is easier than lifting it up or down.

Page 37

1. wheel and axle; 2. pulley; 3. gear; 4. pulley; 5. gear; 6. wheel and axle

Page 38

Answers will vary but may include: 1. plastic, metal, glass; 2. Try to use a mug or a glass. 3. Give the clothing to someone who can use it. Cut up the clothing to use as rags. *Word Alert!* 4. use again; 5. make something seem new again; 6. fill again

Page 39

Answers spell *design*.

Page 40

1. recycle; 2. force; 3. pulley; 4. wheel; 5. engineer; 6. inventor; *Message:* You win!

Language Arts

Page 42

Answers will vary but may include: 1. The haiku is about the sound of flowing water in a brook. 2. A; 3. Dark clouds overhead; 4. Answers will vary but may include rain, a bird, the ocean; 5. Drawings and answers will vary.

Page 43

1. unwise: not wise; 2. teacher: someone who teaches; 3. reuse: to use again; re + use; 4. quietly: in a way that is quiet; quiet + ly; 5. un (prefix) + fair + ly (suffix); 6. A prefix is added before a word, and a suffix comes after a word.

Answer Key

Page 44
1. synonyms; 2. antonyms; 3. antonyms; 4. synonyms; 5. synonyms; 6. antonyms; 7. antonyms; 8. synonyms; *Look It Up!* Answers will vary but may include that the prefix *ant-* means "opposite," and antonyms have opposite meanings.

Page 45
1. watched-verb, game-noun; 2. dancers-noun, twirled-verb; 3. cats-noun, stretch-verb, yawn-verb; 4. mother-noun, is-verb, teacher-noun; 5. house-noun, sits-verb, hill-noun; *Challenge!* Answers will vary but may include that a verb is a thing, and a thing is a noun.

Page 46
1. P; 2. S; 3. S; 4. S; 5. S; 6. P; 7. S; 8. P; 9. S; 10. P; *Challenge!* woman, house, dog, rabbit, penny, bush, glass, dress, chair, wolf

Page 47
Answers will vary but may include (1) Yes, a noun names a person, a place, or a thing. It can also name an idea. (2) A proper noun begins with a capital letter. (3) A proper noun names a particular person, place, or thing. (4) No, the breed of dog is not usually capitalized. (5) Missy is the name of a particular dog, so it's a proper name. If the common noun *mischief* is a dog's name, it becomes a proper noun. *Challenge!* Answers will vary.

Page 48
Answers will vary but may include: *Place*: hilly, rocky, sunny, haunted; *Person*: tall, skinny, angry, smart; *How you run*: quickly, fast, slowly; *How you eat*: politely, messily, quickly

Page 49
1. facts; 2. facts; 3. opinions; 4. opinions; 5. facts; Answers will vary but may include: 6. The neighborhood girls play baseball. 7. The neighborhood girls are sure to beat the neighborhood boys this year.

Page 50
1. Mama, Andy, and Allie Mouse; 2. "Pizza!" He sounds excited. 3. Mama is speaking. The words are in the same paragraph with "said Mama." *Second activity*: Answers will vary.

Page 51
Answers will vary but may include: 1. noisy and out of order, context clue; 2. very cold, context clue; 3. plant scientists, definition; 4. fast sailing ships of long ago, definition; 5. really dislike; context clue; *Word Alert!* Answers will vary but may include: If you want to define a new word, look for its definition in a dictionary.

Page 52
Answers will vary but may include: 1. Yes, it comes from an author's imagination. 2. No, they are listed in alphabetical order. 3. Yes, it could give facts about butterflies. 4. No, nonfiction is true. 5. Yes, otherwise it would be difficult to find words. 6. No, a fiction book does not have an index. 7. Yes, because more information is needed about the facts in a nonfiction book. *Word Alert!* Answers will vary but may include that nonfiction is not fiction—it is true.

Page 53
1. B; 2. A; 3. B; 4. A; 5. A

Page 54
1. proofread; 2. draft; 3. sequence; 4. audience; 5. publish; 6. edit, revise; 7. homophones; *Look It Up!* Drawings will vary but might show a draft of a written work, the effects of a draft of air, and a draft animal.

Page 55
Answers spell *revise*.

Page 56
1. homophones; 2. sequence; 3. synonyms; 4. suffix; 5. plural; 6. opinion; *Riddle and answer:* How is the letter *k* like flour? (You can't make cake without it!)

Social Studies
Page 58
Students use this page to assess their knowledge of *human rights*. Encourage students to explain how their drawings help them remember word meanings.

Page 59
Drawings and answers will vary.

Page 60
1. century; 2. century; 3. decade; 4. decade; 5. century; 6. millennium; *Look It Up!* Answers will vary but may include *cent, centimeter, centipede, centennial,* and *centigrade.*

Page 61
1. Independence Day; 2. Memorial Day; 3. Labor Day; 4. Independence Day; 5. Memorial Day; *Word Alert!* Students should underline *commemorate.* Answers will vary but may include: to remember and honor an important event.

Page 62
1. native; 2. explorers; 3. colonists; 4. settlement; 5. Explorers; *Word Alert!* 6. colonists; 7. explorers; 8. settle

Answer Key

Page 63
Answers will vary but may include: 1. No, it is usually noisy and lively with parades and crowds. 2. Yes, stories are passed down from parents to children over the years. 3. No, a myth is fiction, although it may have an adventure in it. 4. Yes, everyday people told the stories long ago. 5. Yes, people have religious practices, holidays, and ways of cooking and eating. 6. Answers will vary.

Page 64
1. B; 2. A; 3. B; 4. A; 5. B; *Challenge!* Answers will vary but may include: Today we know about the art, the buildings, the beliefs, and the rulers of the large society of people who lived long ago in Mexico and Central America. They were called the Maya people. We know about them because of scientists who have dug up objects from buried cities.

Page 65
1. ancient; 2. customs; 3. explorer; 4. folktale; 5. colonist; 6. rights; 7. decade; *Answer to riddle:* a sponge

Page 66
Answers spell *happen.*

Geography

Page 68
Students use this page to assess their knowledge of *environment.* Encourage students to explain how their drawings help them remember word meanings.

Page 69
1. weather; 2. climate; 3. climate; 4. climate; 5. weather; 6. climate; 7. weather; 8. weather; 9. Answers will vary but may include that the weather is hot and mostly dry in summer, with afternoon thunderstorms. It is chilly and dry in winter.

Page 70
1. grasslands; 2. desert; 3. deserts; 4. grasslands; 5. desert; 6. desert; *Word Alert!* Answers will vary but may include that a grassland is a land in which grass is the main plant.

Page 71
1. B; 2. A; 3. A; 4. B; 5. A; *Look It Up!* Answers will vary but may include: 1. compare weights; 2. measure distances on a map; 3. are its outer layer

Page 72
Names of Continents: Asia, North America, Europe, Antarctica, Australia, South America, Africa; *Places in North America*: Canada, Greenland, United States, Mexico, Caribbean Islands, Central America

Page 73
1. equator; 2. Southern; 3. Northern; 4. South Pole; 5. North Pole; 6. Drawingd will vary but should include vocabulary labels.

Page 74
1. B; 2. A; 3. B; 4. A; 5. A; *Challenge!* Yes, the same city could be the capital for the state and the center of government for its own county.

Page 75
Answers will vary but may include: 1. No, sea level is at an elevation of zero. 2. No, a valley could be formed by a river that is far from a mountain. 3. Yes, it is a way to pass through land. 4. Yes, a river valley may have rich soil for farming. *Word Alert!* An elevated train runs on tracks above the ground.

Page 76
1. cliff; 2. mesa; 3. landforms; 4. peninsula; 5. cliff; 6. mesa; 7. island; *Word Alert!* plain; An airplane flew over flat land.

Page 77
1. A; 2. A; 3. B; 4. A; 5. A; 6. A

Page 78
Answers spell *desert.*

Page 79
ACROSS 1. continent; 4. weather; 5. coastal; 6. kilometer; 7. plain; DOWN 2. elevation; 3. valley; 5. crops

Civics and Economics

Page 81
Answers will vary but may include: *What*: showing respect for other people's beliefs and behaviors; *Importance*: People get along better. They treat each other fairly. They do not force others to act a certain way. *How shown by government*: No laws force people to go to a particular church. People are not punished for believing as they wish. *Opposite*: prejudice, hatred, intolerance

Page 82
1. illegal; 2. legal; 3. legal; 4. legal; 5. illegal; 6. illegal; *Word Alert!* 1. not legal; 2. not perfect; 3. not complete

Page 83
1. import; 2. exported; 3. import; 4. imported; 5. exports; *Challenge!* Students' drawings may show arrows or a scale to suggest a balanced number of imports and exports.

Answer Key

Page 84
Answers will vary but may include: 1. teachers and dentists; 2. shoes, furniture; 3. customer; 4. like their products and buy more of them. 5. Workers who produce things are consumers whenever they buy things.

Page 85
Answers will vary but may include: 1. that a school office is a room, but an office that someone holds is a position. 2. the principal and the teachers. 3. make decisions and vote on laws in ways that will help the voters. 4. to tell the office holder about a problem they would like a solution for such as fixing roads. *Word Alert!* office, official, officers

Page 86
1. A; 2. A; 3. A; 4. A; 5. B; 6. A

Page 87
Answers will vary but may include: 1. buses and subways; 2. police officers; 3. benefits; 4. should work; 5. sanitation; 6. pay for; 7. mayor; 8. public service

Page 88
1. B; 2. A; 3. B; 4. A; 5. A; 6. B

Page 89
1. currency; 2. economy; 3. barter; 4. exchange; 5. exchange; *Look It Up!* Provide students with an advanced dictionary for this activity.

Page 90
Answers will vary but may include: 1. Yes, human rights belong to all people, and civil rights belong to citizens. 2. Yes, we have to go to school and obey laws. 3. Yes, paying taxes is obeying the law. 4. No, civil rights have to do with fairness and justice. 5. No, every country grants citizenship to people who were born there or who become citizens there.

Page 91
Answers will vary but may include: 1. elect lawmakers who will govern them. 2. the state government to obey the national law. 3. on laws about taxes, education, other public services, war, and other matters. 4. share their views and vote the way they would if they were making laws. 5. where and how would millions of people meet to discuss the issues? Direct democracy could only work for small communities.

Page 92
Answers spell *profit*.

Page 93
1. tolerance; 2. consumer; 3. civil; 4. citizenship; 5. legal; 6. legislature; *Riddle and answer:* The more you take from it, the bigger it gets. What is it? (a hole)

Art

Page 95
Students use this page to assess their knowledge of *animation*. Encourage students to explain how their drawings help them remember word meanings.

Page 96
Answers will vary but may include: *What*: a show of a work of art for an audience; *Kinds*: music, dance, comody, drama, gymnastics; *Describing words*: exciting, lively, suspenseful, entertaining, funny; *Why important*: Share good times; appreciate beauty; admire skill; enjoy music; enter a new world

Page 97
1. Students should label the long bar *vertical* and the crossed bar *horizontal*. 2. E; 3. Answers will vary but may include windowsill, top of desk. 4. Answers will vary but may include flagpole, long side of door. 5. Drawings will vary. *Look It Up!* Answers will vary but may include that the horizon is the horizontal line between sky and water or sky and land.

Page 98
1. warm color; 2. warm color; 3. cool color; 4. cool color; 5. cool color; 6. warm color; 7. warm color; 8. cool color

Page 99
Answers will vary but may include: 1. arms; 2. balance; 3. leaps; 4. one leg; 5. to the music; *Challenge!* Possible answers include *arabesque, en pointe, jeté, pas de deux*.

Page 100
1. A; 2. A; 3. B; 4. A; 5. B; *Word Alert!* They all name things with three parts or members.

Page 101
1. still life; 2. seascape; 3. cityscape; 4. landscape; 5. landscape (or seascape); *Challenge!* Drawings will vary.

Page 102
Answers will vary but may include: 1. No, a chorus is a group. 2. No, you cannot hum more than one note at a time. 3. No, a melody is made of notes. 4. Yes, a tempo can be fast, slow, or in between. 5. Yes, a concert is a musical performance.

Page 103
Answers spell *beauty*.

Page 104
ACROSS 2. chorus; 5. vertical; 6. position; 8. animation; DOWN 1. performance; 3. seascape; 4. warm; 7. trio

Notes